LawExpress
INTERNATIONAL LAW

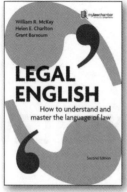

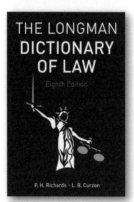
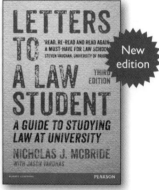

INTERNATIONAL LAW

2nd edition

Stephen Allen
Senior Lecturer in Law, Queen Mary, University of London

Law Express

PEARSON

Harlow, England • London • New York • Boston • San Francisco • Toronto • Sydney • Auckland • Singapore • Hong Kong
Tokyo • Seoul • Taipei • New Delhi • Cape Town • São Paulo • Mexico City • Madrid • Amsterdam • Munich • Paris • Milan

Pearson Education Limited
Edinburgh Gate
Harlow CM20 2JE
United Kingdom
Tel: +44 (0)1279 623623
Web: www.pearson.com/uk

First published 2013 (print and electronic)
Second edition published 2015 (print and electronic)

© Pearson Education Limited 2013, 2015 (print and electronic)

Contains public sector information licensed under the Open Government Licence (OGL) v2.0.
www.nationalarchives.gov.uk/doc/open-government-licence.

Pearson Education is not responsible for the content of third-party internet sites.

ISBN: 978-1-292-01277-3 (print)
      978-1-292-01334-3 (PDF)
      978-1-292-01798-3 (ePub)
      978-1-292-01314-5 (eText)

British Library Cataloguing-in-Publication Data
A catalogue record for the print edition is available from the British Library

Library of Congress Cataloging-in-Publication Data
Allen, Stephen, author.
    International law / Stephen Allen, Senior Lecturer in Law, Queen Mary, University of London. -- Second edition.
        pages cm. – (Law express)
    Includes index.
    ISBN 978-1-292-01277-3 (pbk.)
    1. International law--Outlines, syllabi, etc.   I. Title.
    K559.A49 2015
    341--dc23
                            2014005209

10 9 8 7 6 5 4 3 2 1
18 17 16 15 14

Print edition typeset in 10/12pt Helvetica Neue LT Std by 35
Print edition printed and bound in Malaysia (CTP-PPSB)

NOTE THAT ANY PAGE CROSS REFERENCES REFER TO THE PRINT EDITION

Contents

Supporting resources

Visit the *Law Express* series companion website at **www.pearsoned.co.uk/ lawexpress** to find valuable student learning material including:

- A **study plan** test to help you assess how well you know the subject before you begin your revision
- Interactive **quizzes** to test your knowledge of the main points from each chapter
- Sample **examination questions** and guidelines for answering them
- Interactive **flashcards** to help you revise key terms, cases and instruments
- Printable versions of the **topic maps** and **checklists** from the book
- **'You be the marker'** allows you to see exam questions and answers from the perspective of the examiner and includes notes on how an answer might be marked
- **Podcasts** provide point-by-point instruction on how to answer a typical exam question

Also: The companion website provides the following features:

- Search tool to help locate specific items of content
- E-mail results and profile tools to send results of quizzes to instructors
- Online help and support to assist with website usage and troubleshooting

For more information please contact your local Pearson Education sales representative or visit **www.pearsoned.co.uk/lawexpress**

Acknowledgements

I would like to thank everyone who has reviewed draft chapters of this book. Their comments have been invaluable to the development of the book in its present form. I must acknowledge the tremendous contribution that Christine Statham and Donna Goddard at Pearson, have made to the production of this book. Their support and enthusiasm have been significant factors in the success of this project.

Stephen Allen
Queen Mary, University of London

Publisher's acknowledgements

Our thanks go to all reviewers who contributed to the development of this text, including students who participated in research and focus groups which helped to shape the series format.

Introduction

International law is a popular subject which attracts large numbers of students. However, students often struggle with a number of its substantive topics. In part, this is because international law is very different from most other subjects that most students will have encountered. Many legal subjects (e.g. contract law) exist within a national law framework. Their rules are contained within recognised sources of law (e.g. in a statute), produced by established institutions whose authority to create law is unquestioned (e.g. Parliament). Such rules are liable to be enforced by the courts. In short, a national legal system is a hierarchical legal system. In sharp contrast, international law regulates relations between States and it recognises that all States are equal and sovereign. The international legal system does not have a central legislature nor a court endowed with compulsory jurisdiction to resolve legal disputes. In essence, it is a horizontal legal system. Consequently, international law is a very different kind of 'law' from national law and the fundamental differences between the discrete areas of national law and international law can prove to be quite challenging for students. These differences can impact on any analysis of the nature of the international legal system; they can make it difficult to identify when international law has been created or changed; and they can make it difficult to identify and interpret international legal rules.

As a result, students face significant challenges in answering assessment questions in this subject. Questions often focus on theoretical legal issues. This book helps you to answer such questions, first, by highlighting the abstract issues that have shaped the subject. Second, it identifies the subject's pervasive themes so that you can understand discrete topics in a wider context. Finally, the book uses a range of innovative devices to provide you with strategic advice on how to recognise problematic aspects of international law and how best to tackle them.

Another challenge that international law presents to students is the fact that its various topics are closely interrelated. An assessed question will often involve a number of discrete topics. Accordingly, you will need to acquire a sound knowledge of a wide range of topics and you will also need to understand how they relate to each other. This book advises you on the best way to enhance your technique of answering assessed problems and essay questions. It shows you how to identify the applicable law; how to construct relevant arguments by reference to the most appropriate legal sources; and how to relate the discrete topics of international law to one another in a structured and coherent manner.

However, you should appreciate that the present book is no substitute for a good textbook. It enables you to consolidate and make sense of your learning. It offers you a concise account of the subject's key topics with the aim of providing you with targeted advice on how to improve your performance in assessed work by introducing you to a number of tried and tested revision methods and tips that will help you on the road to success.

📖 REVISION NOTE

Use this book alongside your recommended textbook and the applicable primary sources (international instruments and cases).

International law topics are closely related and so it is important that you revise the whole syllabus of your international law module in order to give yourself the best opportunity of answering assessed questions well.

International law is quite different from any of the legal subjects that you have studied before. You should be sensitive to the unique challenges that it poses for international law as a form of 'law' and the implications that its unusual legal character has for assessed questions in this subject.

Before you begin, you can use the study plan available on the companion website to assess how well you know the material in this book and identify the areas where you may want to focus your revision.

Guided tour

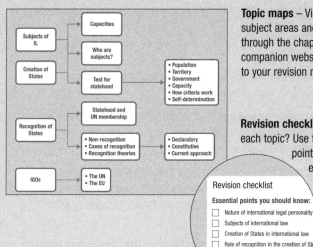

Topic maps – Visual guides highlight key subject areas and facilitate easy navigation through the chapter. Download them from the companion website to pin on your wall or add to your revision notes.

Revision checklists – How well do you know each topic? Use these to identify essential points you should know for your exams. But don't panic if you don't know them all – the chapters will help you revise each point to ensure you are fully prepared. Print the checklists off the companion website and track your revision progress!

Revision checklist

Essential points you should know:
- [ ] Nature of international legal personality
- [ ] Subjects of international law
- [ ] Creation of States in international law
- [ ] Role of recognition in the creation of St
- [ ] International legal personality of IGOs

Sample questions with answer guidelines – Practice makes perfect! Read the question at the start of each chapter and consider how you would answer it. Guidance on structuring strong answers is provided at the end of the chapter. Try out additional sample questions online.

Sample question

Could you answer this question? Below is a typical problem question that could arise on this topic. Guidelines on answering the question are included at the end of this chapter, whilst a sample essay question and guidance on tackling it can be found on the companion website.

Assessment advice – Not sure how best to tackle a question on a particular topic? Wondering what you may be asked? Use the assessment advice to identify the ways in which a subject may be examined and how to apply your knowledge effectively.

ASSESSMENT ADVICE

Essay questions

Essay questions are popular in relation to particular issues such as the creation of States in international law or the doctrines concerning recognition. They often focus on the differences between legal theory and practice. They require students to have a good level of understanding of the relevant legal doctrines and the various case examples.

Key definitions – Make sure you understand essential terminology. Use the flashcards online to test your recall!

KEY DEFINITION: International legal personality

'A subject of the law is an entity capable of possessing international rights and duties and having the capacity to maintain its rights by bringing international claims.'
Reparations Case (1949) ICJ Rep 174.

Key cases and key instruments – Identify and review the important elements of the essential cases and legal instruments you will need to know for your exams.

KEY INSTRUMENT

Article 1, Montevideo
The State as a person of
(a) permanent population
(b) defined territory;
(c) government; and
(d) the capacity t

KEY CASE

The Aaland Islands Case (1920) LNOJ Special Sup. No. 3, 3
Concerning: a territorial dispute between Sweden and Finland

Facts
An International Committee of Jurists had to decide on the legality of Finland's break away from the Russian Empire and its subsequent accession to statehood as a matter of international law.

Legal principle
The Committee observed that a constituted State did not exist until a stable political organisation had been created, and until the public authorities had become strong

Make your answer stand out – This feature illustrates sources of further thinking and debate where you can maximise your marks. Use them to really impress your examiners!

✓ Make your answer stand out

States which have recognised Kosovo have preferred not to express the legal basis for their decision. Is Kosovo a case of self-determination? Do you think that States are worried about the potential for the right of self-determination to be used as a means of dissolving federal States? Does the case of Kosovo demonstrate the overt political nature of recognition? Kosovo is not a UN member. Russia would use its veto in the UNSC if Kosovo made an application for admission. Can it be a State without this status? See Weller (2008).

Exam tips – Feeling the pressure? These boxes indicate how you can improve your exam performance when it really counts.

EXAM TIP

It is important to remember that, traditionally, international law was not concerned with the internal affairs of sovereign States. States were considered to be free to choose their own domestic institutional arrangements (e.g. see Art. 2(7) UN Charter). Consequently, under established international law, States are not bound to adopt democratic governmental practices. Nevertheless, you should consider the extent to which democratic practices might strengthen a claim of statehood.

Revision notes – Get guidance for effective revision. These boxes highlight related points and areas of overlap in the subject, or areas where your course might adopt a particular approach that you should check with your course tutor.

REVISION NOTE

The above principles are not the only fundamental principles of international law. We will be discussing other such principles in this book. However, it is worthwhile refreshing your memory by reading Article 2, UN Charter and the UN Declaration on Friendly Relations and the Principles of International Law (1970). Also, see Figure 1.1.

Don't be tempted to . . . – This feature underlines areas where students most often trip up in exams. Use them to spot common pitfalls and avoid losing marks.

! Don't be tempted to . . .

Don't confuse the topic of recognition of States with recognition of governments. While these areas share certain concepts they are different in important respects.

READ TO IMPRESS

Brownlie, I. (1982) 'Recognition in Theory and Practice', 53 *BYIL* 197.

Craven, M. (1995) 'The European Community Arbitration Commission on Yugoslavia', *BYIL* 66, 333.

Crawford, J. R. (2006) *The Creation of States in International Law*, 2nd edn. Oxford University Press.

Schwarzenberger, G. (1976) *International Law*. Sweet & Maxwell.

Weller, M. (2008) *Contested Statehood: Kosovo's Struggle for Independence*. Oxford University Press.

Read to impress – Focus on these carefully selected sources to extend your knowledge, deepen your understanding, and earn better marks in coursework as well as in exams.

Glossary – Forgotten the meaning of a word? This quick reference covers key definitions and other useful terms.

Glossary of terms

The glossary is divided into two parts: key definitions and other useful terms. The key definitions can be found within the chapter in which they occur as well as in the glossary below. These definitions are the essential terms that you must know and understand in order to prepare for an exam. The additional list of terms provides further definitions of

Guided tour of the companion website

 Book resources are available to download. Print your own **topic maps** and **revision checklists**!

 Use the **study plan** prior to your revision to help you assess how well you know the subject and determine which areas need most attention. Choose to take the full assessment or focus on targeted study units.

 'Test your knowledge' of individual areas with quizzes tailored specifically to each chapter. **Sample problem and essay questions** are also available with guidance on writing a good answer.

 Flashcards test and improve recall of important legal terms, key cases and instruments. Available in both electronic and printable formats.

'You be the marker' gives you the chance to evaluate sample exam answers for different question types and understand how and why an examiner awards marks.

Download the **podcast** and listen as your own personal Law Express tutor guides you through answering a typical but challenging question. A step-by-step explanation on how to approach the question is provided, including what essential elements your answer will need for a pass, how to structure a good response, and what to do to make your answer stand out so that you can earn extra marks.

All of this and more can be found when you visit **www.pearsoned.co.uk/lawexpress**

Table of cases and instruments

◼ Cases

Instruments

TABLE OF CASES AND INSTRUMENTS

The nature of international law

1

Revision checklist

Essential points you should know:

- [ ] Basic structure of the international legal system
- [ ] Foundational principles of international law
- [ ] Whether international law really is a form of 'law'
- [ ] Functions of a legal system
- [ ] Whether the international legal system is an effective legal system

■ Topic map

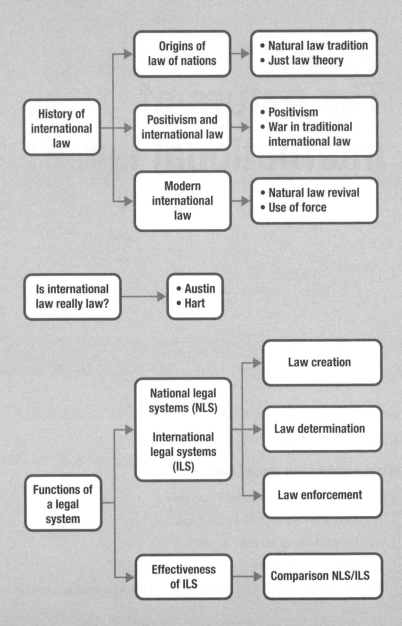

A printable version of this topic map is available from **www.pearsoned.co.uk/lawexpress**

■ Introduction

International law exists to regulate international society. International society is very different from any national society. Consequently, it should come as no surprise to you that the legal systems which regulate these societies are different as well. This chapter discusses the implications of these differences for international law.

ASSESSMENT ADVICE

Questions on this topic often take the form of essay questions. This is a result of the unique characteristics of the international legal system, which have led some to question whether international law is really a form of law. These doubts have generated enquiries into the theoretical foundations of international law. Students need to acquire a good understanding of the nature of law. It is also helpful to appreciate how the international legal system works in practice and to identify appropriate cases which demonstrate international law's effectiveness.

■ Sample question

Could you answer this question? Below is a typical essay question that could arise on this topic. Guidelines on answering the question are included at the end of this chapter, whilst another sample essay question and guidance on tackling it can be found on the companion website.

ESSAY QUESTION

'A legal system grounded in the will of its subjects, that does not possess a centralised legislature or effective means for its enforcement cannot be a form of law at all.' Discuss.

■ International law and international society

Before the founding of the United Nations in 1945, **international law** was largely concerned with the rights and obligations of States. It worked on the assumption that States would look after the interests of their own citizens. Much has changed since this time but States still play a central role in the creation, interpretation and application of international law.

KEY DEFINITION: International law

'International law may be described as a body of rules and principles that determine the rights and duties of states primarily in respect of their dealing with other states and the citizens of other states.' Lowe (2007), 5.

International society was conceived as a political society organised on a non-hierarchical basis with States constituting its members (or basic units). This society provided a way for independent States to coexist in an unstable world and international law was developed to maintain international society. It did this by recognising and protecting the sovereignty of States; and by regulating a number of limited common aims that had been agreed by States and were consistent with international society's nature.

📖 REVISION NOTE

An account of the history of international law is beyond the scope of this book. However, it is a good idea to find out more about how and why international law evolved. See Bull (2002).

The foundational principles of the international legal system are:

- sovereign authority (that all States possess supreme legal authority within their own territory); and

- sovereign equality (all States have equal status within the international legal system).

KEY CASE

The Lotus Case (1927) PCIJ Series A, No. 10

Concerning: criminal jurisdiction regarding a collision on the High Seas
Legal issue: that international law is created by the consent of States

Facts

A French ship collided with a Turkish ship on the High Seas. The collision caused the Turkish ship to sink, and it resulted in the loss of life. The French ship sailed to a Turkish port where a French Officer was charged with manslaughter by the Turkish authorities.

Legal principle

The main question for the Court was whether Turkey's exercise of jurisdiction amounted to a violation of international law. However, it made the following observations on the nature of international law:

The rules of law binding upon States . . . emanate from their own free will as expressed by the conventions or by the usages generally accepted as expressing principles of law and established in order to regulate the relations between these co-existing independent communities or with a view to the achievement of common aims. (at 18)

The '*Lotus* principle' holds that international law is the product of the free will of States. International law cannot be created without the consent of States and it cannot be imposed upon them. Consequently, the actions of States are presumed to be lawful unless they have been specifically prohibited by international law.

📖 **REVISION NOTE**

> The idea that international law is based on the consent of States is explored in Chapter 2.

The principles of State sovereignty and sovereign equality continue to underpin the international legal system today.

The principle of State sovereignty is expressed in:

- Article 2(4), UN Charter: 'All Members shall refrain in their international relations from the threat or use of force against the territorial integrity or political independence of any State, or in any other manner inconsistent with the Purposes of the United Nations.'

- Article 2(7), UN Charter: 'Nothing contained in the present Charter shall authorize the United Nations to intervene in matters which are essentially within the domestic jurisdiction of any State or shall require the Members to submit such matters to settlement under the present Charter . . .'

The principle of sovereign equality is contained in:

- Article 2(1), UN Charter: 'The Organization is based on the principle of sovereign equality of all its Members.'

The above principles were elaborated upon in the UN Declaration on the Principles of International Law concerning Friendly Relations and Co-operation Among States in Accordance with the Charter of the United Nations (GA Res. 2625, 1970). This Declaration subsequently acquired the status of **customary international law (CIL)**.

📖 **REVISION NOTE**

> The above principles are not the only fundamental principles of international law. We will be discussing other such principles in this book. However, it is worthwhile refreshing your memory by reading Article 2, UN Charter and the UN Declaration on Friendly Relations and the Principles of International Law (1970). Also, see Figure 1.1.

Figure 1.1

Key principles of international law

Key principles	Authority	Source
1 State sovereignty	Article 2(7), UN Charter Principle 6, GA Res. 2625 (1970) *Lotus Case* (1927)	Treaty CIL PCIJ (subsidiary means)
2 Sovereign equality	Article 2(1), UN Charter Principle 6, GA Res. 2625 (1970) *Lotus Case* (1927)	Treaty CIL PCIJ (subsidiary means)
3 Prohibition on the use of force	Article 2(4), UN Charter Principle 1, GA Res. 2625 (1970) *Nicaragua Case* (1986)	Treaty CIL ICJ (subsidiary means)

Source: Article 38(1) ICJ Statute

Key developments in international law in the UN period

International law does not just exist to regulate inter-State relations. International Governmental Organisations (IGOs) and individuals now have certain rights/obligations in international law (see Chapter 4).

It is possible to claim that international law is based on universal values and it has a moral purpose which exists beyond inter-State considerations. Recent developments that support a purposive view of international law include:

- the recognition of universalist concepts of 'war crimes' and 'crimes against humanity' developed during the Nuremberg and Tokyo War Trials after the Second World War;

- the Universal Declaration of Human Rights (1948) identified a range of fundamental human rights and obligations;

- the development of a comprehensive range of multilateral human rights **treaties** (see below);

- the development of multilateral treaties concerned with protecting the global environment (e.g. the Framework Convention on Climate Change (1992) and the Kyoto Protocol (1997));

- the creation of extensive regional legal systems, which protect human rights (see below);

- the establishment of the International Criminal Court (ICC), which has jurisdiction to adjudicate on a number of serious international crimes (see below);

- the development of a category of peremptory norms (*jus cogens* and obligations *erga omnes*) (see Chapter 2).

Make your answer stand out

If international law is derived from the consent of States acting together then it could be argued that international law can be whatever States want it to be. On this (positivist) view, international law has no moral basis or purpose. Plenty of scholars have challenged this interpretation. In order to answer assessment questions which focus upon the theoretical foundations of international law you should acquire a good grasp of positivism, the natural law tradition (which claims that law is fundamentally connected to morality) and the Kantian theory (which adopts a purposive view of international law based upon human reason). See Hart (1994); Bull (2002).

◼ Is international law really 'law'?

If all States possess sovereign authority and are equal, how is international law imposed upon them if they violate its rules?

Austin (1790–1859)

Austin defined 'law' as a body of general commands made by a sovereign authority. These commands were backed up by the threat of sanction (enforcement). For Austin, a sovereign authority exists when:

- ◼ it is habitually obeyed by the bulk of the population of the society in question; and
- ◼ it is not in the habit of obeying any other sovereign.

Austin concluded that international law could not amount to a form of law because no overarching sovereign authority exists in the international society of States. Austin's work is discussed in Hart (1994).

Hart (1907–1992)

According to Hart, the members of any society obey legal rules because they have learned to observe them through various social processes as a matter of habit. For him, law's binding quality was *not* derived from its capacity for enforcement. Hart claimed that all legal systems are constituted by a body of primary and secondary rules. Primary rules establish legal standards of behaviour within a society. Secondary rules are needed to provide the foundations of a legal system. They identify the methods by which primary rules can be introduced, changed and enforced.

Hart argued that the international legal system does not have secondary rules because it does not have:

- a central legislature;
- a court endowed with compulsory jurisdiction; or
- a fundamental secondary rule that provides for the identification of all international legal rules (a 'rule of recognition').

While Hart believed that international law *does* exist, he thought that it was a basic form of law rather than a developed legal system (like modern national legal systems).

In contrast, the editors of *Oppenheim's International Law* (1992) claim that international law is a form of law because it is accepted by the members of the international community (States) and because it is enforced by 'external power' (e.g. by the UN Security Council (UNSC) in certain situations (see below)).

📖 REVISION NOTE

The issue of whether international law is really a form of law requires a good understanding of the nature of law itself. It is a good idea to consult a student textbook on jurisprudence for this purpose. See Penner (2008) and D'Amato (1985).

■ The functions of a legal system

KEY DEFINITION: *Ubi societas, ubi jus*

There can be no society without law.

'Law can only exist in a society, and there can be no society without a system of law to regulate the relations of its members with one another.' Brierly (1963), 41.

Any legal system must be able to provide institutional machinery for:

- creating law;
- determining what the law is; and
- enforcing the law.

National legal systems

National legal systems possess a hierarchical (or vertical) structure. The State has sovereign authority within its jurisdiction. The relationship between a State's national law and individuals (or other legal persons) present within its jurisdiction is one of subordination.

- The constitution identifies the sources of national law.
- The Executive and Legislature work together to develop and establish particular national laws.

- Legal officials have the authority to bring alleged wrongdoers before the national courts.
- Courts possess compulsory jurisdiction to decide legal disputes.
- Judicial decisions are enforced by State institutions.

International legal system

Law creation

Because the international legal system lacks the hierarchical structure that characterises national legal systems it cannot be imposed upon States. The international legal system does not have a legislature which has the authority to create and alter international law. Instead international law is made through decentralised law-making processes (principally via treaties and the development of customary international law (CIL)).

However, during the UN era, there have been concerted efforts to codify (to consolidate the various fragments of customary law into a single code) CIL rules by the conclusion of multilateral treaties. In Resolution 174(II)(1947), the UN General Assembly established the International Law Commission (ILC) with the aim of undertaking studies 'to encourage the progressive development of international law and its codification'. The ILC has been responsible for developing draft Conventions in many areas of international law. For instance, its 1966 draft Convention on the Law of Treaties formed the basis of the Vienna Convention on the Law of Treaties (1969). Further, it is becoming increasingly common to view certain multilateral treaties as 'law-making' instruments (see Chapter 2).

> **!** Don't be tempted to . . .
>
> Don't make the mistake of assuming that treaties create *general* international law per se. Treaties will only be legally binding upon those States that are parties to them. However, the provisions of certain treaties may become legally binding upon non-parties if they achieve the status of customary international law. (See Chapter 2.)

Many treaties have been developed with the intention of creating general international law. They do this by aiming to secure near universal **ratification** of the treaties in question by States. Examples include:

- International Covenant on Civil and Political Rights (ICCPR) (1966) – ratified by 166 States.
- International Convention on the Elimination of All Forms of Racial Discrimination (ICERD) (1965) – ratified by 173 States.
- Convention on Biological Diversity (1992) – ratified by 193 States.
- Marrakesh Agreement (the founding treaty of the World Trade Organization (WTO)) (1994) – ratified by 153 States.

In the light of the above, it could be argued that the existing methods of creating international law are well suited to the nature of international society.

Law determination

'Law determination' refers to the identification of the applicable law in the context of a particular issue or dispute. Typically, in a national legal system, the law can be determined by consulting a particular form of the relevant sources of law identified by the national constitution. However, in the international legal system, the absence of a central legislature means that we first have to establish whether international law actually exists on a given issue.

For example, if the international law governing a specific issue arises from a treaty, we must ask whether the provisions of a given treaty bind a particular State. Did the State in question ratify the treaty? If so, what international legal rules did the treaty create?

This task is made all the more difficult because:

- States have considerable scope to interpret international law for themselves (auto-interpretation);
- international legal rules are often quite abstract in nature when compared with those found in national legal systems.

This difficulty is compounded by the international legal system's relatively underdeveloped court structure.

Judicial decisions inevitably clarify the scope and content of legal rules. National legal systems invariably have extensive and elaborate court systems. In contrast, until very recently, international courts seldom had the opportunity to identify and clarify the rules of international law.

There has been a dramatic increase in the number and authority of International Governmental Organisations (IGOs) since the founding of the UN system. IGOs may have the capacity to make international law (depending on the provisions of their constituent treaties). The work of IGOs has substantially developed and reinforced the content of international law (see Chapter 2).

The absence of an international court, which possesses compulsory jurisdiction to decide international legal disputes, coupled with a lack of other international tribunals, has arguably hindered the development of international law. However, since the end of the Cold War (1989), the number of judicial and quasi-judicial bodies with the jurisdiction to resolve disputes between States, between States and individuals and to apply international law against individuals has grown immensely. The increasing 'judicialisation' of international law has meant that international legal rules and principles are being determined authoritatively and with greater frequency.

Law enforcement

States cannot be compelled to submit their legal disputes to international courts. Moreover, until the UN era, no international body had a monopoly on the use of coercion which could be used to enforce international law (in comparison with the coercive powers available to a State to enforce its national law within its own jurisdiction). The absence of established mechanisms for the enforcement of international law seems to cast doubt on whether international law is really law at all.

✎ EXAM TIP

If you are confronted with the question of whether international law is really a form of law you could argue that the concept of law cannot be reduced to questions of enforcement and you should discuss Hart's work in this respect (see above). Further, as *Oppenheim* suggests, international law exists because: States have accepted it as binding upon them; and it is capable of being enforced by 'external power' (e.g. the UN Security Council or by international courts).

The UNSC is charged *inter alia* with the maintenance of international peace and security (Art. 24, UN Charter). Although it is principally a political body, it can enforce international legal rights and obligations by a variety of means, including via the use of force if international peace and security is being jeopardised (Chapter VII, UN Charter). The way that the UNSC responded to Iraq's invasion of Kuwait demonstrates the capacity to enforce international law when serious breaches occur (see Chapter 10).

You could add that the growing 'judicialisation' of international law reinforces the idea that international law is being enforced by bodies that are external to States (see Chapter 9).

✎ EXAM TIP

Questions that invite you to discuss whether international law is a form of law often prompt students to reflect upon the nature of law by reference to national legal systems. However, international law is unlike national law. States can interpret and apply international law for themselves. And, in certain situations, States may enforce international law directly (the 'self-help' method). You should consider the extent to which the nature of international law influences our concept of law in general.

Figure 1.2

Functions of the international legal system

Law creation (Art. 38(1) ICJ Statute)	Treaties CIL General principles
Law determination	Auto-interpretation International organisations Courts
Law enforcement	UN Security Council Courts Self-help

The effectiveness of international law

It is important that the members of any society accept the validity of the legal system which governs their society as a means of regulating their dealings with one another. If there is no such acceptance then it is virtually impossible to conclude that a particular society exists at all. If the members of a society accept the validity of their legal system then the 'law habit' can flourish.

There is considerable evidence to show that States regard themselves to be bound by international law. This must be true otherwise international society would not function and we would soon notice. For example, the international postal service, international travel, communication and commerce are all heavily dependent upon the existence of an effective international legal system.

While States may dispute the precise content of international law, they rarely claim that they are not bound by it. For example, when Iraq invaded and annexed Kuwait in 1990, it did not claim that it was free to disregard the international law protecting State sovereignty. Instead, it argued that its actions were justified in international law (it claimed that it was reunifying the ancient Iraqi nation which had been dismembered by the European colonial powers). Accordingly, it claimed to be acting in accordance with international law. However, the claim was not accepted by the international community of States. (See Chapter 10.)

You could consider the extent to which international law's effectiveness depends upon the political legitimacy bestowed upon States when they comply with international law (or the withholding of legitimacy where a State chooses to disregard international law). This approach would allow you to show how international law influences international relations beyond the courtroom.

However, international law has experienced numerous high profile failures, for example:

- NATO's Intervention in Kosovo (1999) (see Chapter 10).
- The US/UK-led invasion of Iraq (2003) (see Chapter 10).

The above examples should cause us to reflect on the extent to which contemporary international law discharges all its responsibilities. However, they should not distort our view of whether international law exists at all.

Comparing international and national legal systems

Is the test of enforcement or effectiveness a fair measure of the binding quality of law? It is often assumed that national laws are enforced. However, we all know that not all national laws are observed or enforced. Many individuals routinely violate national criminal laws (e.g. driving with excess speed). Further, we accept that not all serious criminal offences will be prosecuted. National laws are sometimes ineffective (such as the ban on the underage drinking of alcohol). However, the practical shortcomings of national legal systems do not lead us to question whether national law exists. We understand the legal validity of national law on any given issue is independent of the capacity of the State to enforce it.

Because international society is structured in a very different way from national societies, the legal system that seeks to regulate it will inevitably differ as well. The notion of sovereign equality renders the enforcement machinery typically found in national legal systems deeply problematic and potentially harmful if it were to be applied to international society. Arguably, the comparisons between the international legal system and national legal systems are unfair and unhelpful.

■ Putting it all together

Answer guidelines

See the essay question at the start of the chapter.

Approaching the question

- Identify the characteristics of the international legal system (ILS).
- Compare the above characteristics with those of national legal systems (NLS).
- Consider various theories about law.
- Discuss the key international legal doctrines, institutional practices and cases which show how the ILS performs the functions of a legal system.

Important points to include

- Identify and discuss the characteristics of the ILS:
  - ☐ International law is created by the consent of States.
  - ☐ The principles of State sovereignty and sovereign equality.
  - ☐ That the ILS does not possess a central legislature and a court endowed with compulsory jurisdiction (and explain why this is the case).
  - ☐ Explain the difficulties of enforcing international law by non-judicial means.
- Compare the characteristics of the ILS with those of NLS. The latter have:
  - ☐ Central legislatures; courts which possess compulsory jurisdiction to apply the law; and institutional machinery to enforce national law effectively.
- ILS has the institutional machinery to create international law:
  - ☐ States develop and agree multilateral treaties that are 'law making' in character.
  - ☐ The provisions of UN General Assembly resolutions can create CIL. ▶

- International law is increasingly becoming more court-centred. The number of judicial bodies endowed with special jurisdiction is growing (e.g. the ICC).
- UNSC has the power to enforce international law in situations that threaten international peace and security (under Chapter VII, UN Charter).
- States accept international law as binding upon them and they typically observe its rules and principles.

 Make your answer stand out

You should reflect upon the theoretical issues raised by the question:

- Hart showed that effective enforcement is not a central requirement for law to exist.
- Hart demonstrated that law's binding quality is largely a psychological matter arising from a sense of obligation. States accept that they are bound by international law and there is no doubt that it 'exists'.
- The fact that international law is created by the consent of its subjects is not problematic. National laws are indirectly created by the consent of the governed.

READ TO IMPRESS

Brierly, J. L. (1963) *The Law of Nations*, 6th edn. Oxford University Press.

Bull, H. (2002) *The Anarchical Society: A Study of Order in World Politics*, 3rd rev. edn. Columbia University Press.

D'Amato, A. (1985) 'Is International Law Really "Law"?', 79 *Northwestern University Law Review* 1293.

Hart, H. L. A. (1994) *The Concept of Law*, 2nd rev. edn. Oxford University Press.

Jennings, R. and Watts, A. (eds) (1992) *Oppenheim's International Law*, 9th edn. Oxford University Press.

Lowe, V. (2007) *International Law*. Oxford University Press.

Penner, J. E. (2008) *McCoubrey & White's Textbook on Jurisprudence*, 4th edn. Oxford University Press.

www.pearsoned.co.uk/lawexpress

 Go online to access more revision support including quizzes to test your knowledge, sample questions with answer guidelines, podcasts you can download, and more!

Sources of
international law

2

Revision checklist

Essential points you should know:

☐ Formal sources of international law

☐ How the sources are used to enable international legal rules to develop

☐ How the sources relate to each other

☐ Role of IGOs in the creation of international law

☐ Distinction between 'soft law' and 'hard law'

■ Topic map

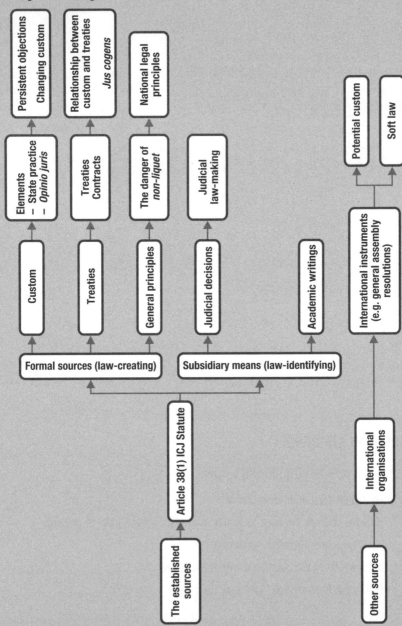

A printable version of this topic map is available from **www.pearsoned.co.uk/lawexpress**

■ Introduction

How is international law made and how can we identify its rules? In a typical national legal system these questions are answered easily. The national constitution will establish the methods by which laws are created and the law in a given area can be discovered by consulting the applicable source of law (e.g. a statute). However, international law is different for the reasons outlined in Chapter 1. To recap, international law has three fundamental characteristics:

- ■ States create international law – the principle of sovereign equality means that international law cannot be imposed on States.
- ■ There is a no central legislative body responsible for creating international law.
- ■ There is no international court with compulsory jurisdiction to determine or enforce international law.

These differences often make it difficult to identify the rules of international law and how they came into being. This is sometimes known as the sources problem.

ASSESSMENT ADVICE

Essay questions

This is an area where reflective questions are often asked about how the sources work together to provide the international legal system with coherence or how they develop international law. You need to know how the various sources relate to each other and so it is important that you learn the whole topic.

Problem questions

Problem questions often focus on a legal dispute concerning the existence of a new State practice that challenges an established rule of customary international law (CIL). They require students to explain the means by which CIL is created and how it can be changed. Treaty provisions may shape a new CIL rule and so you will need to have a good understanding of how the sources interrelate. It is important that you approach such questions in a methodical and systematic way. Keep your discussion of the relevant sources separate before you explain how they work together for the benefit of international law.

■ Sample question

Could you answer this question? Below is a typical essay question that could arise on this topic. Guidelines on answering the question are included at the end of this chapter, whilst a sample problem question and guidance on tackling it can be found on the companion website.

ESSAY QUESTION

How do treaties and customary international law work together to develop general international law?

■ The sources problem

International law's nature means that the sources of international law are much more diverse than those found in national legal systems. International law evolves directly through the conduct of States. International lawyers must distinguish between those types of State activity that will create international law from those which will not. In addition, international lawyers must be able to identify the precise legal rules that such behaviour has created.

☐ REVISION NOTE

It is widely believed that international law is created by the consent of States. If you bear this in mind, you will be able to make sense of this topic. Keep asking yourself the following question: could the actions of States be seen as evidence of an intention to create international law?

■ Established sources of international law

KEY INSTRUMENT

Article 38(1), ICJ Statute (1945)

'The Court, whose function is to decide in accordance with international law such disputes as are submitted to it, shall apply:

(a) international conventions, whether general or particular, establishing rules expressly recognised by the contesting States;

(b) international custom, as evidence of a general practice accepted as law;

(c) the general principles of law recognised by civilised nations;

(d) subject to the provisions of Article 59, judicial decisions and the teachings of the most highly qualified publicists of the various nations, as a subsidiary means for the determination of rules of law.'

- You should note that the Statute of the International Court of Justice (ICJ) is an international treaty annexed to the UN Charter.

- Article 38(1) is a direction to the ICJ. However, it has been widely accepted as an authoritative statement concerning the formal sources of international law.

- The sequence of sources listed in Article 38(1) does not establish a hierarchy of sources. However, the sequence is important in practice (see below).

> **! Don't be tempted to . . .**
>
> Don't be tempted to learn only part of this topic. The sources often work together to develop general international law and so you will need to develop your understanding of the whole topic.

Customary international law (CIL)

The origins of international law are found in customary international law (CIL) and it is the default source in the absence of applicable treaty law.

> **KEY DEFINITION: Customary international law (CIL)**
>
> CIL has been defined as 'a constant and uniform usage, accepted as law' (*Asylum Case* (1950) ICJ Rep 266, 277).

CIL is well suited to the decentralised structure of the international legal system because it enables international law to evolve directly from the conduct of States.

The elements of CIL: state practice and *opinio juris*

State practice (material element)

Any State activity can constitute State practice for the purpose of creating CIL. Examples include: official public statements, physical actions, diplomatic correspondence, treaty-making, national legislation and the conduct of States in International Governmental Organisations (IGOs). However, for State practice to form the basis of a CIL rule much will depend on the circumstances of a given case and the nature of the legal issue in question.

Certain conditions must be satisfied if the practice is to be capable of providing the basis for a CIL rule:

- State practice must be extensive. A significant number of States, including those States whose interests would be specially affected by the creation of a CIL rule, need to participate in the practice. State practice must be 'both extensive and uniform' (*North Sea Continental Shelf Cases* (1969)); and

- State practice should amount to a consistent pattern of behaviour. It should be 'generally consistent' (*Nicaragua Case* (1986)); and

- a sufficient period of time must have passed in order to show that the above conditions are satisfied.

Opinio juris (the psychological element)

KEY DEFINITION: *Opinio juris*

It is necessary that States believe that they are under a legal obligation to follow a particular practice.

KEY CASE

North Sea Continental Shelf Cases (1969) ICJ Rep 3
Concerning: the delimitation of the continental shelf
Legal issue: the nature of opinio juris

Facts

Article 6, Continental Shelf Convention (1958) provided that, in the absence of agreement or special circumstances, claims would be determined by the equidistance principle. Germany was not a party to the Convention. Denmark and the Netherlands claimed that Article 6 reflected the CIL position and that Germany was bound by the CIL rule.

Legal principle

The ICJ noted that, in order for CIL to form, there must be: 'evidence of a belief that this practice is rendered obligatory by the existence of a rule of law requiring it. The need for such a belief, i.e. the existence of a subjective element, is implicit in the very notion of *opinio juris sive necessitates*. The States concerned must therefore feel that they are conforming to what amounts to a legal obligation.'

The requirement that State practice is accepted as law is vitally important as it is impossible to distinguish between practices which arise from habit or courtesy ('usages') and those practices which States are legally obligated to follow. But how do we prove that States feel bound to follow a particular practice? States are artificial legal persons (see Chapter 4). They act through national governments which rarely make their intentions clear. Where evidence of the intentions of particular States is unclear the instruments of IGOs may reveal whether States in general consider themselves under a legal obligation to behave in a certain way. For example:

■ In the *Nicaragua Case* (1986), the ICJ decided that the provisions of UN Declaration on the Principles of International Law concerning Friendly Relations (GA Res. 2625 (XXV) (1970)) could be used to satisfy the *opinio juris* required to support the existence of a CIL rule concerning the prohibition on the use of force.

The persistent objector rule

The **persistent objector rule** operates thus: if a State objects to a new CIL rule from the moment the rule is established and it maintains its objection the State will not be bound by that particular CIL rule.

KEY CASE

Anglo-Norwegian Fisheries Case (1951) ICJ Rep 116

Concerning: the delimitation of Norway's territorial waters

Facts

UK challenged Norway's use of the straight baseline method for measuring the extent of its territorial sea. It claimed that a 10-mile closing line for bays was an established CIL rule. Norway's practice meant that it claimed a substantially larger territorial sea than other States.

Legal principle

ICJ rejected the UK's claim by reference to the persistent objector rule. It held that:

'In any event the . . . rule would appear to be inapplicable as against Norway, in as much as she has always opposed any attempt to apply it to the Norwegian coast.'

EXAM TIP

The persistent objector rule provides an important example of the role of State consent in the creation and operation of international law. It is a good idea to connect its operation to the foundations of international law.

 Make your answer stand out

Why can't a State object to an established CIL rule if international law is founded on the notion of State consent? You should consider the limits of the consent model of international law. Is international law created by establishing that particular States have consented to a CIL rule or is it created by the presence of consensus on the part of States in general? See Akehurst (1974–5).

The role of IGOs in creating international law

The authority of certain IGOs has developed significantly since 1945, when Art. 38(1) came into force. Subsequent developments have shown the limits of the narrow approach to the sources of international law adopted in that provision. IGOs generate a considerable number of instruments, resolutions, guidelines, recommendations etc. Many of these international instruments are political or technical in nature but some of them are capable of creating international law.

UN General Assembly Resolutions

The UN General Assembly (UNGA) is principally a political body and it does not have direct legislative authority. In other words, it cannot create international law by itself. However, many General Assembly Resolutions (GA Res.) have influenced the development of international law because often political and legal objectives are linked in the international legal system.

In particular, they may contribute to the creation of a CIL rule:

■ The provisions of a GA Res. may show that States consider themselves to be legally bound, obligated to follow a certain practice (satisfying the *opinio juris* requirement). For example, in the *Nicaragua Case*, the ICJ held that certain provisions of the UN Declaration on Friendly Relations (GA Res. 2625 (XXV) (1970)) demonstrated the existence of the *opinio juris* required to support a prohibition on the use of force in international law.

■ State activity in voting for a GA Res. and statements made in the General Assembly may amount to evidence of State practice. For example, the provisions of the UN Declaration of Legal Principles Governing the Activities of States in the Exploration and Use of Outer Space (GA Res. 1962 (XVII) (1963)) prohibited sovereign claims over celestial bodies. It was adopted without dissent and State activity in this context was widely regarded as amounting to State practice that could support the creation of a new CIL rule preventing States from making sovereign claims to celestial bodies, such as the Moon.

 Make your answer stand out

GA Res. 1962 (XVII) (1963) established both the *opinio juris* and State practice elements needed to create the CIL rule discussed above. How can CIL be created by such limited evidence of State practice? Can such resolutions create CIL directly? Can CIL be created instantly? See the International Law Association's Report (2000).

Changing CIL

KEY DEFINITION: Custom (changing CIL)

'Custom is . . . established by virtue of a pattern of claim, absence of protest by states particularly interested in the matter at hand and acquiescence by other states.' Shaw (2008), 89.

Conduct that is contrary to an established CIL rule will amount to a breach of international law and it could give rise to State responsibility (see Chapter 8). Much depends on how interested States react to a contrary practice. If they protest against it then their objections confirm the established CIL rule. However, if they accept the contrary practice by deciding not to react to it such inactivity may be interpreted as evidence of acquiescence (implied consent) and it could support the formation of a new CIL rule.

📖 REVISION NOTE

The State seeking to establish a new rule, in effect, makes an offer to other States suggesting that an existing CIL rule should be changed and States then decide whether to accept or reject it. If they accept it a new CIL rule will be created; if they reject it, the established CIL remains applicable. See Lowe (2007) at 39.

You should remember that any change to established CIL rules will require a thorough assessment of whether there is enough support from States for the new CIL rule and that will depend on the nature of the rule in question. For example, it would be easier to introduce a new CIL relating to State jurisdiction in outer space than to alter the rules concerning the use of force in international law.

 Make your answer stand out

CIL requires that States must feel as though they are under an existing legal obligation to follow a particular practice (the *opinio juris* element). How can the CIL position be changed if the new practice is contrary to the established CIL rule? If a State engages in a practice which violates international law, how can the *opinio juris* requirement be satisfied and a new CIL rule established? Should this requirement be ignored in such situations? Should it be presumed to exist? Does it depend on the importance of the new practice for the international community? This issue is explored by the ICJ in the *North Sea Continental Shelf Cases* (1969). Also see Akehurst (1974–5).

■ Treaties

KEY DEFINITION: Treaties

Treaties are legally binding agreements that commit the parties to follow a particular course of conduct by reference to rights and/or obligations.

Treaty law will be considered further later in this text (Chapter 3). Here we are only concerned with treaties as a source of international law.

Types of treaty

'Treaty contracts' are often bilateral agreements or involve a small number of States. They are usually concerned with technical or commercial matters. They create rights and obligations for State parties in a very similar way to the way that contracts agreed between ordinary legal persons do.

'Law-making treaties' are invariably multilateral agreements designed to establish or develop international law on a range of issues. While they may create rights and obligations for State parties, law-making treaties exist within the framework of international law. Arguably, they possess quasi-legislative character and have the potential to develop CIL (see below).

📖 REVISION NOTE

You must remember that treaties only bind those States that are parties to them (as they have given their express consent to the terms contained in the treaty).

The relationship between treaty law and CIL

If certain conditions are fulfilled, particular treaty provisions can influence CIL.

KEY CASE

North Sea Continental Shelf Cases (1969) ICJ Rep 3
Concerning: the delimitation of the continental shelf
Legal issue: how treaty provisions can contribute to the development of CIL

Facts
See above.

Legal principle
The ICJ stated that treaty provisions can inform CIL in three ways:

(i) they can codify CIL on a particular issue. In such a situation, a treaty simply clarifies existing CIL;

(ii) they can help to create new CIL;

(iii) they can inspire new CIL rules (but the necessary elements of State practice and *opinio juris* will need be satisfied for a new CIL rule to emerge).

! Don't be tempted to . . .

You should not assume that treaty provisions will necessarily generate new CIL rules as a matter of course. A number of conditions must be satisfied before this can occur. See below.

In the *North Sea Continental Shelf Cases* (1969), the ICJ set out a number of conditions that must be established before a treaty provision can create new CIL:

- the relevant treaty provisions should be fundamentally law creating in character (they should be 'normative'); and

- there must be very widespread and representative participation in the State practice which must be supported by those States whose interests would be specially affected by the treaty provisions in question; and

- State practice must be extensive and virtually uniform in support of the new CIL rule in the period since the treaty in issue was adopted.

✎ EXAM TIP

The requirement that State practice must be extensive and uniform was relaxed by the ICJ in the *Nicaragua Case* (1986) where it held that State practice must be widespread and consistent. You should think about the reasons why the ICJ changed its view in this case. Could it be that the ICJ recognised that the approach adopted in the *North Seas Continental Shelf Cases* was too restrictive and that it reduced this source's capability to contribute to the development of international law? Does the subsequent, more relaxed approach have any consequences for the view that international law is created by State consent?

You should note the following points in situations where treaty provisions contribute to new CIL rules:

- A State that is not a party to the treaty concerned is not made accountable to that treaty.

- The rights and/or obligations of a State that is not a party to the treaty will flow from CIL.

- Ordinarily, a State that is a party to a treaty which creates CIL will derive its rights and/or obligations from that treaty and not from CIL.

Treaties and CIL have equal authority in international law (*Wimbledon Case* (1923)). Consequently, where CIL and treaty law cover the same issue both sources will coexist. In such a situation treaty law will prevail (in practice) but the CIL rule will not disappear. If the treaty becomes inapplicable for some reason then the CIL rule may be applied instead.

KEY CASE

Nicaragua Case (Merits) (1986) ICJ Rep 14

Concerning: responsibility for paramilitary activities against Nicaragua
Legal issue: the relationship between CIL and treaties in international law

Facts

The US made a declaration which sought to restrict the ICJ's jurisdiction to decide a case concerning responsibility for paramilitary activities in Nicaragua. It stated that treaty law was inapplicable to the dispute. Consequently, the relevant provisions of the UN Charter could not be invoked in the case.

Legal principle

The ICJ decided that the declaration constituted a valid reservation to the ICJ's jurisdiction (see Chapter 9). However, it held that it had jurisdiction over the case because the dispute was governed by CIL as well as treaty law.

Jus cogens

Jus cogens (or peremptory norms) of international law are those rules that have acquired a higher status in international law because they are widely seen as being of fundamental importance to the international legal system. States are not allowed to enter into treaties that seek to change (or ignore) rules that have become *jus cogens*.

KEY INSTRUMENT

Article 53, Vienna Convention on the Law of Treaties (VCLT) (1969)

'A treaty is void if, at the time of its conclusion, it conflicts with a peremptory norm of general international law . . . a peremptory norm of general international law is a norm accepted and recognised by the international community of States as a whole as a norm from which no derogation is permitted . . .'

The category of *jus cogens* highlights the way in which the international community seeks to protect its key values through international law.

> ## ! Don't be tempted to . . .
>
> Don't make the mistake of assuming that all fundamental international legal rules have attained *jus cogens* status (and therefore they can't be modified by treaties). Peremptory status is very exceptional, as discussed below.

This superior status of *jus cogens* norms does not mean that they can never be changed. It is important that change should be allowed to occur in order for international law to reflect the core values of the international community. However, Article 53 VCLT makes it clear that they cannot be changed easily. Peremptory norms: 'can be modified only by a subsequent norm of general international law having the same character'. In other words, they can only be changed by the development of a new peremptory norm.

Rules such as the prohibitions on slavery and genocide are certainly *jus cogens*. There is authority to suggest that the following are also peremptory:

■ the prohibitions on the use of force (*Nicaragua Case* (1986));

■ the prohibitions on the use of torture (*Furundzija Case* (1998));

■ the right of self-determination (*East Timor Case* (1995)).

However, the fundamental nature of this category means that very considerable evidence will be required for a rule to become peremptory and courts have been careful not to develop this category as a result.

Peremptory norms derive their normative force from CIL and so they demonstrate not only the limits of treaties as a source of international law, but they also show that, in certain circumstances, CIL can have priority over treaty law.

Further, you should be aware that the contents of Article 38(1) derive their binding force from CIL (because although these rules are contained in a treaty, technically they only amount to a direction to the ICJ on how to apply international law to the cases that come before it). However, you should remember that treaty law and CIL are mutually supportive and that they interact extensively in order to clarify and develop general international law.

Figure 2.1

Relationship between treaties and custom

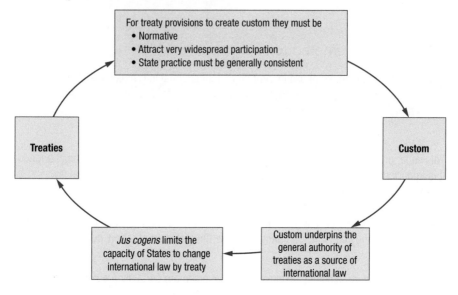

For treaty provisions to create custom they must be
- Normative
- Attract very widespread participation
- State practice must be generally consistent

Treaties

Custom

Jus cogens limits the capacity of States to change international law by treaty

Custom underpins the general authority of treaties as a source of international law

■ General principles of law

> **KEY DEFINITION: General principles of law**
>
> Article 38(1)(c) ICJ Statute: 'the general principles of law recognised by civilised nations.'

The danger of *non-liquet*

While an established body of legal rules may be able to resolve the vast majority of legal disputes, what happens when a court is confronted with a new legal issue which is not covered by existing rules? In such a case there is a danger that it would have to decline jurisdiction because no applicable law exists. This situation is known as ***non-liquet***.

Shared national legal principles

Article 38(1)(c) can be seen as an attempt to create a category of general principles which are commonly found in *national* legal systems in order to avoid a situation of *non-liquet*. Examples include:

- adoption of the circumstantial evidence rule in the *Corfu Channel Case* (1949);
- use of the principle of estoppel in the *Temple of Preah Vihear Case* (1962);
- recognition of the concept of a limited company in the *Barcelona Traction Case* (1970).

Article 38(1)(c) is not restricted to general principles shared by *national* legal systems. It also encompasses general principles of *international* law. However, most of the latter have secured CIL status and are thus supported by Article 38(1)(b) instead.

■ Judicial decisions

Article 38(1)(d) operates subject to Article 59, ICJ Statute. It provides that: 'The decision of the Court has no binding force except between the parties and in respect of the particular case.'

This means that the ICJ does not operate according to the doctrine of *stare decisis* or judicial precedent (decisions in previous cases are binding in subsequent cases on the same points of law) which is entrenched in many national legal systems. However, the ICJ does strive for consistency, which is an important element in authoritative decision making.

According to Article 38(1)(d), judicial decisions are 'a subsidiary means for the determination of the rules of law'. They are not formal sources of international law – they do not create international law – instead, they identify the international law in question (the applicable treaty law, CIL or general principles).

Judicial law making

Judges are not supposed to make the law but the distinction between law identification and law creation is often blurred in practice. It is widely believed that judicial decisions may create international law. For example, judicial decisions can bring about the existence of new rules of international law by:

- establishing a rule for the purpose of measuring the extent of the territorial sea (*Anglo-Norwegian Fisheries Case* (1951));

- recognising an IGO's legal personality (*Reparations Case* (1949) (see Chapter 4));

- judicial decisions can be counted as evidence of State practice for the purpose of creating CIL.

Article 38(1)(d) encompasses decisions made by all international courts. It includes:

- adjudicative bodies with universal jurisdiction, such as the ICJ and ICC (see Chapter 9);

- regional judicial bodies such as the European Court of Human Rights; and

- specific bodies such as the International Criminal Court for Rwanda.

It also extends to the decisions of national courts. Notable cases which have significantly influenced the development of international law include:

- the *Quebec Secession Case* (1998) decided by the Canadian Supreme Court, which concerned the right to self-determination (see Chapter 7);

- the *Pinochet* litigation (2000) in the English courts, which concerned State immunity (see Chapter 6).

Academic writings

Academic writings are also 'a subsidiary means for the determination of the rules of law' under Article 38(1)(d). Consequently, they are law identifying rather than law creating. Scholars strongly influenced the early development of international law. However, as the doctrine of international law became more established their influence diminished. The writings of modern scholars and practitioners continue to perform the important function of identifying and clarifying international law.

Other sources of international law

The sources included in Article 38(1) are the most important sources of international law. However, international lawyers are increasingly taking notice of a range of sources that are not legally binding in themselves but may help to interpret or develop international law.

Figure 2.2

Relationships between law-creating and law-identifying sources

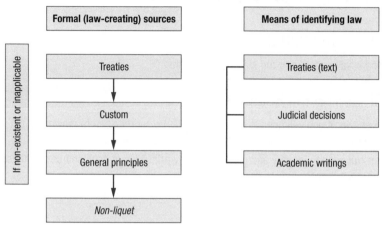

Soft law

UNGA resolutions do not *usually* provide evidence of an intention to create CIL on the part of States. Instead they declare policy goals that States wish to achieve in the future. Particular provisions of a GA Resolution may have the potential to become normative (become law) in time – they may attract the necessary *opinio juris* and State practice to create a new CIL rule eventually. This potential normative force has led to such instruments being called 'soft law'. However, it is important to remember that these instruments are not themselves legally binding. They must be distinguished from the sources of 'hard law' identified in Article 38(1). The same would be true for instruments produced by other IGOs.

Despite the theoretical challenges soft law poses for international law, non-binding international instruments are often legally relevant. They often provide a context in which other legally binding rules can be interpreted.

 Make your answer stand out

Should non-binding international standards be called international law at all? Does the essence of all law flow from its binding quality? You should reflect on the very nature of law itself and so it is important that you link any such discussion back to the themes discussed in Chapter 1. See Boyle and Chinkin (2007).

■ Putting it all together

Answer guidelines

See the essay question at the start of the chapter.

Approaching the question

- To answer it you will need to explain each of the sources before moving on to discuss how they work together to clarify or create international law.
- You will need to identify and discuss the key principles of each source and those principles that regulate their interaction.
- Your work must be supported by appropriate case examples.

Important points to include

- You should start by discussing Article 38(1) which sets out the sources of international law.
- Identify the elements of CIL (State practice and *opinio juris*) and discuss how CIL rules can be established with appropriate case examples.
- Explain how the CIL rules can be changed.
- Outline how treaties are made and explain how they exemplify State consent.
- Compare and contrast the advantages and disadvantages of CIL and treaty law as mechanisms for the development of international law:
  - ☐ CIL directly reflects State behaviour and so it evolves naturally to meet the needs of the international community.
  - ☐ CIL is flexible and it can be dynamic in nature.
  - ☐ CIL rules may be unclear and they usually cannot be developed quickly.
  - ☐ Treaties derive their authority directly from State consent.
  - ☐ Treaties are deliberate agreements that create clear rights and/or obligations for the parties.
- Demonstrate how CIL and treaty law combine together for the benefit of general international law (see the *North Sea Continental Shelf Cases*):
  - ☐ Treaties can clarify CIL; e.g. the provisions of the VCLT codified CIL in this area of law.
  - ☐ Treaties can develop CIL; e.g. the provisions of the UN Convention on the Law of the Sea (1982) developed CIL rules relating to the Exclusive Economic Zone.
  - ☐ Treaties can inspire new CIL.

- You should remember that these sources are distinct and that they operate differently:

  □ It cannot be assumed that treaty provisions will create new CIL. They must be normative and they must enjoy widespread and representative State practice which must have emerged since the treaty was adopted (see *North Sea Continental Shelf Cases* and the *Nicaragua Case*).

- You could discuss the ways in which CIL limits States' ability to modify international law using treaties:

  □ You could analyse *jus cogens* norms which cannot be altered or contradicted by treaty law.

  □ You should explain the importance of Article 53 VCLT and identify appropriate norms that have achieved this status.

  □ You should also discuss the reasons for the existence of this category.

✓ Make your answer stand out

You could reflect on how these sources work together to improve international law's coherence and to contribute to its development against the background of challenges which confront international law (see Chapter 1).

READ TO IMPRESS

Akehurst, M. (1974–75) 'Custom as a Source of International Law', 47 *BYIL* 53.

Boyle, A and Chinkin, C. (2007) *The Making of International Law*. Oxford University Press.

International Law Association (2000) Statement of Principles Applicable to the Formation of General Customary International Law.

Lowe, V. (2007) *International Law*. Oxford University Press.

Shaw, M. N. (2008) *International Law*, 6th edn. Cambridge University Press.

www.pearsoned.co.uk/lawexpress

Go online to access more revision support including quizzes to test your knowledge, sample questions with answer guidelines, podcasts you can download, and more!

Treaties

3

Revision checklist

Essential points you should know:

- ☐ Nature of treaties
- ☐ How treaties are created
- ☐ Concept of reservations
- ☐ How treaties are interpreted
- ☐ Grounds for invalidating and terminating treaties

Topic map

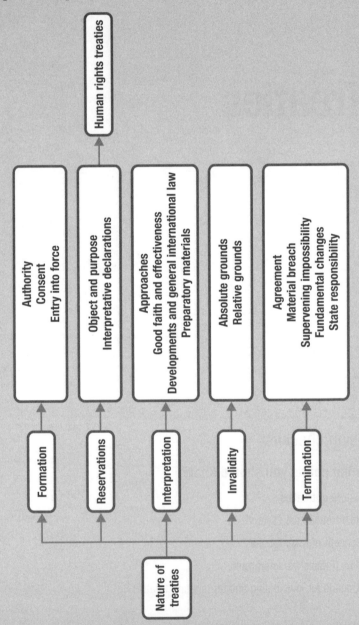

Human rights treaties

Formation
Authority
Consent
Entry into force

Reservations
Object and purpose
Interpretative declarations

Interpretation
Approaches
Good faith and effectiveness
Developments and general international law
Preparatory materials

Invalidity
Absolute grounds
Relative grounds

Termination
Agreement
Material breach
Supervening impossibility
Fundamental changes
State responsibility

Nature of treaties

A printable version of this topic map is available from **www.pearsoned.co.uk/lawexpress**

■ Introduction

Treaties are the most important way of making international law today. It is vital that you acquire a thorough understanding of the legal rules which govern their formation, operation and ending. It is possible to draw certain parallels between contract law and treaty law. There are clear advantages in making this connection. Consent plays an important role in both. However, while this basic parallel provides a helpful starting point for the purpose of understanding treaty law, it gives rise to certain dangers as well. These will be discussed below.

ASSESSMENT ADVICE

Essay questions

Essay questions often focus on a discrete area of treaty law (e.g. reservations or interpretation) and ask you to investigate the differences between theory and practice. You should acquire a good understanding of the key doctrines and how they are implemented. A thorough knowledge of the applicable case law is also important for this purpose.

Problem questions

Problem questions tend to concentrate on the practical application of treaty law. Disputes often focus on legal issues such as reservations, invalidity and breach. It is important that you analyse the legal issues set out in the question. Make sure that you separate your discussion of the various rights and obligations of the States involved and apply the law to the facts.

■ Sample question

Could you answer this question? Below is a typical problem question that could arise on this topic. Guidelines on answering the question are included at the end of this chapter, whilst a sample essay question and guidance on tackling it can be found on the companion website.

PROBLEM QUESTION

Alpha, Gamma, Omega and Ruritania are the original member States of a customs union. The union was created by the Founding Treaty 1995. It provides for the free movement of goods, services, capital and workers within the union. When Gamma ratified the treaty, it made a reservation which excluded any of the treaty's provisions concerning the free movement of workers in respect of the nationals of any State that joined the union after 2005, if Gamma considered that such a restriction was in its national interest. Francovia ratified the Treaty in 2011. Gamma has announced that it will not allow Francovian nationals to work in Gamma. Omega believes that Francovia's position is contrary to the spirit of the treaty. Alpha and Ruritania entered into the Rail Treaty in 2000. It concerned the construction of a railway between Alpha and Ruritania. The railway required the excavation of a tunnel under the Central Mountain Range, an area of outstanding natural beauty. Alpha became concerned that the project was causing substantial environmental harm. Consequently, it decided to halt work on the tunnel for six months to undertake an environmental impact assessment. Ruritania announced that Alpha's actions amounted to a material breach. Ruritania has decided to terminate the treaty. Alpha claims that Ruritania no longer wishes to build the railway due to a global financial crisis. Advise Omega and Alpha.

■ Nature of treaties

Treaties are legally binding agreements that commit the parties to follow a particular course of conduct by reference to rights and/or obligations. Treaty law mirrors contract law in certain respects. States are in a similar position to individuals who have decided to enter into contractual relations in national law. This parallel can also be used to explain the consent model of international law (see Chapters 1 and 2). Treaty law and contract law are also broadly similar in the way that they seek to regulate the creation of agreements, their interpretation, and what happens when agreements are breached.

! Don't be tempted to . . .

Don't make the mistake of assuming that treaties and contracts are the same thing. They are different in fundamental respects:

- States may create international law when they enter into treaties with each other. In contrast, individuals do not make (national) law when they make contracts.

- The multilateral nature of many treaties weakens the analogy with contract law (which is essentially bilateral in nature).

- The consent model of international law cannot fully explain CIL's development (see Chapter 2).

- The connection between treaties and contracts is questionable in relation to human rights treaties (see below).

KEY DEFINITION: Treaties

Article 2(2) of the Vienna Convention on the Law of Treaties (VCLT) (1969) defines a treaty as an: 'international agreement concluded between States in written form and governed by international law'.

VCLT is the most important reference point in treaty law. It codified CIL in many respects.

📖 **REVISION NOTE**

It is important to understand how the main sources of international law, treaties and CIL, relate to each other. You should revise the present topic alongside Chapter 2.

Treaty formation

The term 'treaty' is a general label used to describe a wide range of international agreements. They are sometimes called Conventions, Covenants, Declarations, Statutes, Acts or Protocols. Treaties do not need to be contained in a single document. Much like contracts they can be created through a series of documents (e.g. via exchange of letters). Even the signed minutes of a meeting between State representatives could constitute a treaty in certain circumstances.

KEY CASE

Maritime Delimitation and Territorial Questions Case (1994) ICJ Rep 112

Concerning: whether the ICJ had jurisdiction to decide a sovereignty dispute
Legal issue: how treaties can arise in international law

Facts

A preliminary issue was whether the signed minutes of a meeting between the Foreign Ministers of Qatar and Bahrain, which gave the ICJ jurisdiction over the dispute, were a treaty.

Legal principle

The ICJ held that the particular minutes in question were: 'not a simple record of a meeting . . . They enumerate the commitments to which the Parties had consented. They thus create rights and obligations in international law for the Parties. They constitute an international agreement.'

Authority

Governments act on behalf of States. However, governmental officials must be able to demonstrate that they have the authority to negotiate and conclude treaties:

- Authority can be established if an official produces a document which shows that they have 'full powers' to represent the State in question (Art. 7(1) VCLT).

- 'Full powers' are not required where the Head of State, Head of Government or the Foreign Minister is acting in a representative capacity (Art. 7(2) VCLT). Also see *Cameroon* v *Nigeria* (2002) ICJ Rep 303 (below).

Expressions of consent to be bound

KEY INSTRUMENT

Article 11 VCLT (Consent to be bound)

This provision identifies the ways in which States express their consent to be bound by a treaty. The main forms are by signature and ratification.

Multilateral treaties typically provide that States express their consent to be bound by means of ratification. Signature is more common in bilateral treaties. In situations where ratification is required, signature does not express consent (it only authenticates the text).

The modalities of ratification are matters for each particular State. For example:

- Under Article 2 US Constitution, the President can only ratify treaties that have been approved by at least two-thirds of the Senate.

- UK Parliament had no constitutional role in the conclusion of treaties. However, a constitutional practice (the Ponsonby rule) provides that a signed treaty should be presented to Parliament for 21 days, allowing the opportunity for debate before ratification. This rule is now contained in the Constitutional Reform and Governance Act 2010.

Entry into force

Ratification signals a State's willingness to be bound by a treaty. However, it does not signal the beginning of the legal commitments contained in the treaty. They only arise when the treaty enters into force.

KEY INSTRUMENT

Article 24(1) VCLT (Entry into Force)

'A treaty enters into force in such manner and upon such date as it may provide or as the negotiating States may agree.'

Multilateral treaties typically expressly provide for their entry into force. For example, Article 126, Rome Statute on the International Criminal Court (1998) provided that the treaty would enter into force: 'on the first day of the month after the 60th day following the date of the deposit of the 60th instrument of ratification' with the UN Secretary-General. It entered into force on 1 July 2002.

States that decide to ratify a multilateral treaty after it has entered into force will be bound by its provisions in the event of ratification.

■ Reservations

Treaty reservations encourage States to participate in multilateral treaties by allowing them to modify their treaty commitments in relation to other State parties. Not all multilateral treaties permit reservations and some treaties may only allow them in relation to certain issues. However, in general, reservations are only permitted when they are not incompatible with the object and purpose of the treaty in question. The legal validity of reservations was first considered by the ICJ in the *Reservations Case* (1951). The law in this area was subsequently developed by the VCLT.

KEY INSTRUMENT

Article 19 VCLT (Scope of Reservation)

When signing or ratifying a treaty a State may make a reservation unless:

(a) the reservation is prohibited by the treaty;

(b) the treaty provides only for specified reservations; or

(c) the reservation is *incompatible with the object and purpose of the treaty.*

KEY INSTRUMENT

Article 20 VCLT (Extent of Reservation)

'acceptance by another contracting State of a reservation constitutes the reserving State a party to the treaty in relation to that other State . . .'

KEY INSTRUMENT

Article 21 VCLT (Effect of Reservation)

A reservation:

1. (a) modifies for the reserving State in its relations with that other party the provisions of the treaty to the extent of the reservation;

   (b) modifies those provisions to the same extent for that other party in its relations with the reserving State.

2. The reservation does not modify the provisions of the treaty for the other parties to the treaty inter se.

3. When a State objecting to a reservation has not opposed the entry into force of the treaty between itself and the reserving State, the provisions to which the reservation relates do not apply as between the two States to the extent of the reservation.

Figure 3.1

State A's reservation

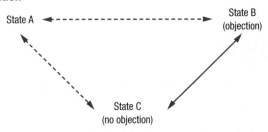

If it is possible to make a valid reservation, the reserving State must notify the other State parties. The parties have 12 months to object to the reservation otherwise they are considered to have accepted it (see Art. 20(5) VCLT).

State A makes a reservation to a multilateral treaty which affects its legal relations with State B and State C. If State B objects to the reservation but State C does not object then:

- State A will become a party to the treaty (Art. 20(4)(a) VCLT).
- The reservation will modify legal relations between State A and State C to the extent of the reservation (Art. 21(1)(a) and (b) VCLT).
- The treaty will govern legal relations between State A and State B in general. However, the treaty provisions affected by the reservation will not come into force between them (Art. 21(2) VCLT).

KEY CASE

Anglo-French Continental Shelf Case **(1977) 54 ILR 6**

Concerning: continental shelf claims in the English Channel

Facts

The UK and France were parties to the Continental Shelf Convention (1958). Article 6 provided that conflicting claims should be determined by the equidistant principle. However, France had made a reservation in relation to Article 6 so far as it could be used to resolve claims in the English Channel. The UK objected to this reservation.

Legal principle

Article 6 could not be used to resolve the dispute in the light of France's reservation to the 1958 Convention pursuant to Article 21(3) VCLT.

📖 REVISION NOTE

What sources of international law were available to the Panel in the *Anglo-French Continental Shelf Case*? It had to rely upon CIL rules to resolve this dispute. See the ICJ's position as stated in the *North Sea Continental Shelf Cases* (1969) on the relationship between treaty law and CIL. (Also see Chapter 2.)

Object and purpose

The ICJ made it clear in the *Reservations Case* (1951) that it was for State parties to decide whether a reservation was incompatible with the object and purpose of a treaty. How can compatibility be assessed?

The *permissibility school* – a reservation should first be scrutinised to determine whether it is compatible with the object and purpose of the treaty. If the reservation is found to be compatible in principle then State parties must decide whether to endorse it. However, if the reservation is incompatible with the treaty it can have no legal effect and a State seeking to make the reservation is bound by the whole treaty.

The *opposability school* – the question of compatibility with the treaty's object and purpose merely assists the State parties in deciding whether to accept the reservation or not. The task of determining the validity of reservations is entirely a matter for the State parties. On this view, a reservation could be accepted by State parties even if it was contrary to the object and purpose of the treaty.

Human rights treaties

The UN Human Rights Committee (HRC), which is the monitoring body for the ICCPR, explained in General Comment 24 (1994) that:

> [Human rights] treaties . . . are not a web of inter-State exchanges of mutual obligations. They concern the endowment of individuals with rights.

Consequently, such treaty commitments should be viewed as pledges rather than reciprocal State rights/obligations. The HRC asserted its right to decide whether a given reservation was compatible with the ICCPR or not. It reaffirmed its position in the *Rawle-Kennedy Case* (2002).

 Make your answer stand out

The HRC's stance on reservations has been strongly criticised by States. In particular, the US, UK and France have claimed that decisions about the validity of reservations are a matter for States. This approach has been confirmed by the International Law Commission. Is the operation of human rights treaties still a matter for States or has the authority to determine compliance with such treaties been handed over to the relevant monitoring bodies? These questions are important because they concern the nature of modern international law. You should analyse the competing views on this issue. Read Pellet (2011).

Interpretative declarations

You should be aware of the distinction between reservations and 'interpretative declarations'. A valid reservation sets out the terms upon which the reserving State is willing to be bound by the treaty. However, an 'interpretative declaration' is a State's interpretation of a particular treaty provision. It does not constitute the terms on which the declaring State has consented to the treaty and it could be disregarded by other States, courts and IGOs.

✎ EXAM TIP

The distinction between a reservation and an 'interpretative declaration' can be a fine one. States sometimes make 'interpretative declarations' that are really disguised reservations. Courts have been willing to disregard them as invalid reservations. See the ECtHR's decision in *Belilos* v *Switzerland* (1988). It is important to be aware of this distinction because declarations have no legal effect and the VCLT's provisions concerning objections to reservations are not applicable in relation to declarations (see Art. 20 VCLT above). Problem questions sometimes include States that make both reservations and declarations so you need to be aware of the differences between them.

■ Treaty interpretation

KEY INSTRUMENT

Article 31 VCLT (Interpretation)

'A treaty shall be interpreted in good faith in accordance with the ordinary meaning to be given to the terms of the treaty in their context and in the light of its object and purpose.'

Different approaches

There are three different approaches to treaty interpretation:

■ the textual approach (objective);

■ the 'intentions of the parties' approach (subjective);

■ the 'object and purpose' approach (purposive).

Article 31, VCLT is formulated in a way that draws upon all of these approaches in an effort to promote the effectiveness of treaties. The ICJ has stated its preference for the textual approach on many occasions. See the *Admissions Case* (1950) ICJ Rep 4. The ICJ reinforced this approach in the *Territorial Dispute (Libya* v *Chad) Case* (1994) ICJ Rep 6, when it observed that: 'Interpretation must be based above all upon the text of a treaty' (Para. 41).

KEY CASE

Territorial Dispute (Libya v Chad) **(1994) ICJ Rep 6**

Concerning: a boundary dispute between neighbouring States
Legal issue: the ICJ's approach to treaty interpretation

Facts

Whether a 1955 treaty concluded between Libya and France (the colonial power then responsible for Chad's territory) established the international boundary between the two territories.

Legal principle

According to the ICJ, the 1955 treaty: 'clearly conveys the intention of the parties to reach a definitive settlement of the question of their common frontiers . . . Any other construction would be contrary to one of the most fundamental principles of treaties, consistently upheld by international jurisprudence, namely that of effectiveness' (Para. 51).

Good faith and effectiveness

In interpreting treaties, courts are guided by the fundamental principles of good faith and effectiveness (see the *Gabcikovo-Nagymaros Case* (1997) below).

KEY INSTRUMENT

Article 26 VCLT (*Pacta Sunt Servanda*)

'Every treaty in force is binding upon the parties to it and must be performed in good faith.'

However, the meaning of a treaty provision may not be obvious and therefore courts may have to consider other methods of interpretation, in appropriate cases. In searching for the best available interpretation, the VCLT authorises courts to draw upon a wide range of sources.

Subsequent developments/general international law

KEY INSTRUMENT

Article 31(3) VCLT

For the purpose of interpreting a treaty, a court may have regard to:

(a) any subsequent agreement between the parties regarding the interpretation of the treaty . . . ;

(b) any subsequent practice in the application of the treaty which establishes the agreement of the parties regarding its interpretation; or

(c) any relevant rules of international law applicable in the relations between the parties.

KEY CASE

Namibia Advisory Opinion **(1971) ICJ Rep 16**

Concerning: the legality of South Africa's presence in Namibia
Legal issue: how treaty interpretation can be modified by subsequent practice

Facts

South Africa was responsible for Namibia under the Mandate system. Its Mandate was revoked and it was instructed to withdraw from Namibia. SC Res. 276 (1970) reaffirmed this position. SC Res. requested an Advisory Opinion on the consequences of South Africa's continued occupation. South Africa argued that the ICJ had no jurisdiction to consider the request because two UNSC permanent members abstained from voting for the resolution. Article 27(3) UN Charter provides: UNSC decisions 'shall be made by an affirmative vote of nine members including the concurring votes of the permanent members . . .'

Legal principle

The ICJ observed that a subsequent practice had evolved that had been 'consistently and uniformly' followed which allowed permanent members to abstain from voting without such conduct constituting a bar to the adoption of a resolution. Article 27(3) was interpreted in the light of subsequent practice as permitted by Article 31(3)(b) VCLT.

 Make your answer stand out

VCLT's recognition of the influence of subsequent agreements/practices on treaty interpretation demonstrates the evolutionary nature of international law. Article 31 VCLT reinforces the idea that specific developments should be interpreted in ways that are consistent with the background rules of international law. You could harness the above examples to demonstrate the coherence and integrity of international law as a whole.

Preparatory materials

KEY INSTRUMENT

Article 32 VCLT

Article 32 VCLT permits courts to have recourse to supplementary materials to confirm the meaning resulting from the application of Article 31; or to determine the meaning when that interpretation:

(a) leaves the meaning ambiguous or obscure;

(b) leads to a result which is manifestly absurd or unreasonable.

Supplementary materials include preparatory works (e.g. treaty drafts, records of negotiation meetings, conference proposals etc.). International courts often referred to preparatory works extensively when reaching their decisions. Examples include:

- *Kasikili/Seddu Islands (Botswana v Namibia) Case* (1999) ICJ Rep 1045;
- *Sovereignty over Pulau Islands (Indonesia v Malaysia) Case* (2002) ICJ Rep 625.

✎ EXAM TIP

Do preparatory works always assist in the task of determining the meaning of the final text? They may not necessarily help because they don't necessarily embody the terms of a final agreement. For example, in the *Maritime Delimitation and Territorial Questions Case* (1994) the ICJ found the preparatory works were an unreliable guide for determining the meaning of the final agreement.

▓ Invalidity

Articles 46–53 VCLT set out the grounds for invalidating treaties. Grounds for invalidity can be divided into two categories:

- Absolute grounds render the treaty void – the treaty is incapable of having any legal effect from the time it was concluded.
- Relative grounds render the treaty voidable – the innocent State has the choice of whether to affirm the treaty or to terminate it.

Absolute grounds	Relative grounds
Coercion (Arts. 51–52)	Error (Art. 46)
Breach of *jus cogens* (Art. 53)	Fraud (Art. 49)
Corruption (Art. 50)	Lack of authority (Art. 46)

KEY INSTRUMENT

Article 53 VCLT (*jus cogens*)

'A treaty is void if, at the time of its conclusion, it conflicts with a peremptory norm of general international law . . .'

📖 REVISION NOTE

The concept of *jus cogens* is explored in Chapter 2.

KEY CASE

Cameroon v *Nigeria* (2002) ICJ Rep 303

Concerning: a territorial/maritime boundary dispute
Legal issue: the binding nature of a Head of State's authority to enter into treaties for the purposes of international law

Facts

Nigeria claimed that a treaty between the two States was invalid because even though it had been signed by Nigeria's Head of State, it did not comply with the requirements of Nigeria's national law.

Legal principle

A Head of State has the authority to conclude a treaty on behalf of his or her State (Art. 7(2) VCLT). Consequently, the resulting treaty obligations cannot be avoided by reference to national law (see Art. 46(1) VCLT).

Termination

Treaties can be terminated in a number of ways:

- agreement;
- material breach;
- supervening impossibility of performance;
- fundamental change of circumstances.

Agreement

If the purpose for which the treaty was created has been achieved then the State parties can agree to bring the treaty to an end. Alternatively, the parties to a treaty may together decide to terminate it before its aims have been achieved (Art. 54 VCLT).

Material breach

Article 60 VCLT regulates situations where a **material breach** arises. For an innocent State to terminate (or to suspend) a treaty the breach by the State in default must be *material*.

KEY DEFINITION: Material breach

Article 60(3) VCLT, a material breach as one that is:

(a) a repudiation of the treaty not sanctioned by the VCLT; or

(b) the violation of a provision essential to the accomplishment of the object or purpose of the treaty.

The consequences of material breach depend on whether the treaty is bilateral or multilateral in nature.

■ A material breach of a *bilateral* treaty entitles the innocent party to terminate or to suspend the treaty or parts of it (Art. 60(1) VCLT).

📖 REVISION NOTE

This position is similar to the position adopted by contract law in response to a breach of a condition.

■ In a *multilateral* treaty, where one State party commits a material breach the innocent State parties can agree to terminate (or suspend) the treaty for all parties or in relation to the defaulting State alone. However, all the innocent State parties must agree upon this course of action (Art. 60(2) VCLT).

KEY CASE

Namibia Advisory Opinion (1971) ICJ Rep 16

Concerning: the legality of South Africa's presence in Namibia
Legal issue: the legal consequences of a material breach of a treaty

Facts

See above.

Legal principle

The ICJ observed that South Africa had committed a material breach of treaty obligations concerning its Mandate over Namibia (as determined by the UNGA in GA Res. 2145 (1966)). In the ICJ's view, this resolution amounted to: 'the exercise of the right to terminate a relationship in a case of a deliberate and persistent violation of obligations which destroy the very object and purpose of that relationship' (at 96).

✎ EXAM TIP

Article 60(2)(a) VCLT provides that a State party that is 'specially affected' by a breach may suspend the operation of the treaty between itself and the defaulting State. You should consider how a State could satisfy the requirement of being specially affected in this context. Is the idea of specially affected States comparable to those States that are specially affected by CIL developments (see Chapter 2)?

KEY CASE

Gabcikovo-Nagymaros Case (1997) ICJ Rep 7

Concerning: liability for the termination of a treaty to construct a dam
Legal issue: the legal consequences of a material breach of a treaty

Facts

In 1977, Hungary and Czechoslovakia entered into a treaty which was concerned with the construction of a dam. In 1989, Hungary abandoned work on the project. Czechoslovakia continued construction work. In May 1992, Hungary notified Czechoslovakia that it was terminating the treaty. It claimed that Czechoslovakia's unilateral construction activities constituted a material breach. In October 1992, Czechoslovakia diverted the river's waters into a bypass canal. The diversion caused substantial environmental harm.

Legal principle

The ICJ decided that Hungary could not invoke a material breach in May 1992 as no breach had occurred at that time. Hungary had not acted in good faith in abandoning its construction work. However, the ICJ held that Czechoslovakia was in material breach (although this only happened in October 1992 when it diverted the river's waters).

Supervening impossibility

KEY INSTRUMENT

Article 61(1) VCLT

'A party may invoke the impossibility of performing a treaty as a ground for terminating or withdrawing from it if the impossibility results from the permanent disappearance or destruction of an object indispensable for the execution of the treaty . . .'

KEY CASE

Gabcikovo-Nagymaros Case (1997) ICJ Rep 7

Concerning: liability for the termination of a treaty to construct a dam
Legal issue: to show the circumstances in which a treaty can be lawfully terminated on the basis that it has become impossible to perform

Facts

Hungary claimed that one of the grounds for terminating the 1977 treaty (the full facts of the case are outlined above) was that it had become impossible to perform because implementing the treaty would cause serious environmental harm. Consequently, it argued that, under Article 61(1) VCLT, an essential object of the treaty had been destroyed.

> **Legal principle**
>
> The ICJ decided that the treaty's performance had been compromised in large part by Hungary's failure to carry out the construction work for which it was responsible under the 1977 treaty. Accordingly, impossibility could not constitute a valid ground for terminating the treaty.

Fundamental change of circumstances

KEY INSTRUMENT

Article 62(1) VCLT

'A fundamental change of circumstances which has occurred with regard to those existing at the time of the conclusion of a treaty, and which was *not foreseen* by the parties, *may not be invoked* as a ground for terminating or withdrawing from the treaty *unless*:

(a) the existence of those circumstances constituted an essential basis of the consent of the parties to be bound by the treaty; and

(b) the effect of the change is radically to transform the extent of obligations still to be performed under the treaty.'

KEY CASE

Fisheries Jurisdiction Case (1973) ICJ Rep 3

Concerning: whether the ICJ had jurisdiction to adjudicate a fisheries dispute

Facts

The UK initiated ICJ proceedings in response to Iceland's decision to extend its exclusive fisheries jurisdiction in violation of a 1961 bilateral treaty. The treaty permitted either party to refer such a dispute to the ICJ. However, Iceland claimed that the court had no jurisdiction and that the treaty was no longer binding upon it because there had been a fundamental change of circumstances since the treaty was concluded.

Legal principle

The ICJ decided that there was no fundamental change of circumstances on the facts. In its view, in order to invoke Article 62 successfully, the change: 'must have increased the burden of the obligations to be executed to the extent rendering performance something essentially different from that originally undertaken'.

KEY CASE

Gabcikovo-Nagymaros Case (1997) ICJ Rep 7

Concerning: liability for the termination of a treaty to construct a dam
Legal issue: when a treaty can be lawfully terminated because a fundamental change of circumstances has occurred

Facts

In addition to its other claims (see above), Hungary argued that it was entitled to terminate the treaty as there had been a fundamental change of circumstances since the treaty was concluded. In particular, it claimed that the obligations contained in the 1977 treaty had been radically transformed by the collapse of communism and the reduced economic benefits associated with the project.

Legal principle

The ICJ held that these developments did not radically transform the obligations contained in the 1977 treaty. It emphasised that not only must the change of circumstance be fundamental, it must also have been unforeseen. The ICJ concluded that: 'the stability of treaty relations requires that the plea of fundamental change of circumstances be applied only in exceptional cases' (Para. 104).

Treaty termination and State responsibility

KEY CASE

Rainbow Warrior Case (1987) 26 ILM 1346

Concerning: State responsibility for a violation of sovereignty
Legal issue: to show the relationship between treaty breaches and State responsibility

Facts

Two French security agents sank the *Rainbow Warrior* within New Zealand's territorial waters. The dispute was settled by a 1985 bilateral treaty in which it was agreed that the agents would be detained in an overseas military base for three years. The agents were repatriated before the agreed period had elapsed. France claimed that the reasons for repatriating the agents were beyond its control (*force majeure*).

Legal principle

France's defence of *force majeure* (a defence to State responsibility under Article 22, Articles on State Responsibility) was not established on the facts.

However, in the *Rainbow Warrior Case*, the Panel observed that:

> the legal consequences of a breach of a treaty, including the determination of the circumstances that may exclude wrongfulness (and render the breach only apparent)

and the appropriate remedies for breach, are subjects that belong to the customary Law of State Responsibility.

In principle, the Panel accepted that the defences to State responsibility could enable a State which had breached a treaty obligation to avoid liability for its actions.

Gabcikovo-Nagymaros Case (1997) ICJ Rep 7

Concerning: liability for the termination of a treaty to construct a dam
Legal issue: the relationship between treaty breaches and State responsibility

Facts

Hungary invoked the defence of necessity to justify its decision to abandon construction work on the dam project. Necessity is a recognised defence to State responsibility (see Chapter 8).

Legal principle

The ICJ acknowledged the relevance of the rules on State responsibility in cases where a State's liability for a material treaty breach was being determined. However, it decided that Hungary could not satisfy the requirements of the defence of necessity on the facts.

Figure 3.2
Material breach

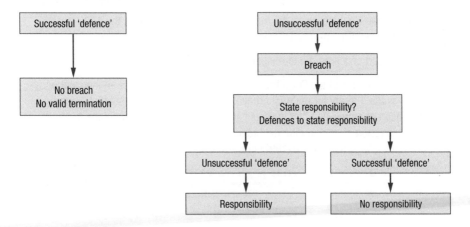

A commits material breach of bilateral treaty with B and B elects to terminate treaty (Art. 60(1) VCLT)

A's 'defences' to treaty breach

Supervening impossibility (Art. 61 VCLT)

Fundamental change of circumstances (Art. 62 VCLT)

■ Putting it all together

Answer guidelines

See the problem question at the start of the chapter.

Approaching the question

The question raises the following key topics:

- how treaties are created;
- reservations;
- how treaties are terminated.

Important points to include

The first part involves consideration of the validity of reservations made in relation to a 1995 multilateral treaty:

- You should discuss how treaties are created.
- You should introduce the concept of ratification.
- You should outline the function of reservations. The *Reservations Case* and the VCLT's provisions should be mentioned at this stage.
- Is Gamma's reservation compatible with the object and purpose of the 1995 treaty?
- You should assess this issue by reference to the *Reservations Case* and Article 19 VCLT. Does the reservation conflict with the purpose of the union?
- Have the other State parties accepted Gamma's reservation? See Article 20 VCLT.
- What are the legal effects of the reservation (if it is valid)? Does the 1995 treaty apply between Gamma and Francovia? See Article 21 VCLT.

The second part concerns the termination of the 2000 bilateral treaty:

- Is Alpha in breach of the 2000 treaty? Article 60(1) VCLT permits an innocent party to terminate a treaty for material breach. Article 60(3) defines 'material breach' as a violation of a provision that is essential to the object or purpose of the treaty. Is the suspension of work a material breach? You should consider cases such as the *Gabcikovo-Nagymaros Case* (1997) in this context.

Make your answer stand out

- Regarding the 1995 treaty, does the lack of objection by the other member States render the reservation valid? This point allows for discussion of the permissibility and opposability schools regarding the effect of reservations.

- Could Ruritania's termination of the 2000 treaty be justified on environmental grounds (or as a result of the global financial crisis)?

- Fundamental change of circumstances (Art. 62 VCLT) – *Fisheries Jurisdiction Case*.

- Supervening impossibility (Art. 61 VCLT) – *Gabcikovo-Nagymaros Case*.

- Could Ruritania justify its decision via State responsibility – *Rainbow Warrior Case* and *Gabcikovo-Nagymaros Case*?

READ TO IMPRESS

Aust, A. (2010) *Modern Treaty Law and Practice*, 2nd edn. Cambridge University Press.

Craven, M. (2000) 'Legal Differentiation and the Concept of the Human Rights Treaty in International Law', 11 *EJIL* 489.

Fitzmaurice, M. (2010) 'The Practical Working of the Law of Treaties', in M. Evans, *International Law*, 3rd edn. Oxford University Press.

Hollis, D. B. (2013) *The Oxford Guide to Treaties*. Oxford University Press.

Pellet, A. (2011) Special Rapporteur's Seventeenth Report, Reservations to Treaties, ILC, 63rd Session. http://untreaty.un.org/ilc/reports/2011/2011report.htm

Shelton, D. (2013) *Oxford Handbook of International Human Rights Law*. Oxford University Press.

www.pearsoned.co.uk/lawexpress

 Go online to access more revision support including quizzes to test your knowledge, sample questions with answer guidelines, podcasts you can download, and more!

International
legal personality

Revision checklist

Essential points you should know:

- [ ] Nature of international legal personality
- [ ] Subjects of international law
- [ ] Creation of States in international law
- [ ] Role of recognition in the creation of States
- [ ] International legal personality of IGOs and individuals

Topic map

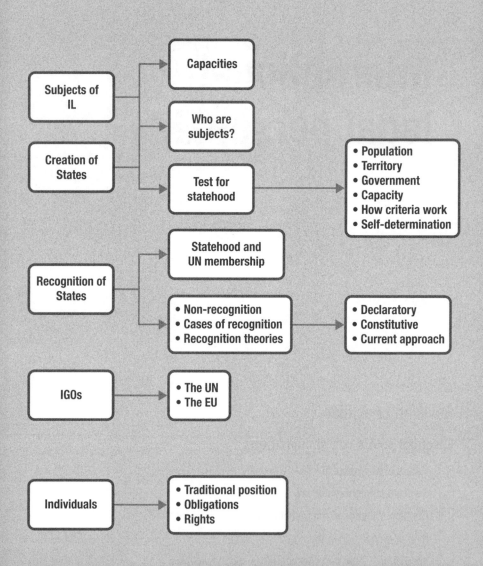

◼ Introduction

Legal personality is a concept shared by all legal systems. It is necessary for legal 'persons' to be able to enforce legal rights and for them to be subject to legal obligations. National legal systems typically recognise the legal personality of individuals – both natural and artificial persons (companies). States are the principal legal persons within the international legal system. But how do political entities achieve statehood? And do only States enjoy legal personality within this system?

ASSESSMENT ADVICE

Essay questions

Essay questions are popular in relation to particular issues such as the creation of States in international law or the doctrines concerning recognition. They often focus on the differences between legal theory and practice. They require students to have a good level of understanding of the relevant legal doctrines and the various case examples.

Problem questions

These questions typically provide a scenario in which a new States has been created. You need to understand the legal rules governing statehood and recognition. There are plenty of case examples in this area. However, the relationship between statehood and recognition is complicated and so you should take care not to confuse these doctrines with one another.

◼ Sample question

Could you answer this question? Below is a typical problem question that could arise on this topic. Guidelines on answering the question are included at the end of this chapter, whilst a sample essay question and guidance on tackling it can be found on the companion website.

PROBLEM QUESTION

Arcadia, a powerful federal State, is in the process of breaking up. A region of Arcadia, known as Beta, is inhabited by ethnic Betans. Betans have long claimed that they have been oppressed by the central government of Arcadia. The Betan political leadership ▶

proclaimed itself to be the legitimate government of the new State of Beta. The government of Arcadia refused to accept the existence of the Betan State. It launched a military offensive against Beta. Fifty small States have decided to recognise the State of Beta. They tabled a UN General Assembly resolution condemning Arcadia's invasion of Beta. The resolution claimed that such action constitutes a violation of the Betan people's right to self-determination. The resolution was controversial but it was adopted by a narrow margin. Beta is preparing to make an application to become a member of the UN. The Arcadian government has resolved to complete its military campaign to regain 'Arcadian territory'. It has announced that it now controls at least half of Betan territory. Further, the Arcadian government signals that it will use its veto power in the UN Security Council to prevent Beta from becoming a UN member. Advise the Betan government whether Beta has become a State under international law.

■ The subjects of international law

KEY DEFINITION: International legal personality

'A subject of the law is an entity capable of possessing international rights and duties and having the capacity to maintain its rights by bringing international claims.' *Reparations Case* (1949) ICJ Rep 174.

Capacities of international legal persons

International legal personality may entitle a **subject of international law** to:

- bring legal claims to enforce international legal rights;
- have the power to make international agreements/treaties;
- enjoy various immunities and privileges;
- be under certain international legal obligations.

Who are the subjects of international law?

KEY DEFINITION: Subjects of international law

'The subjects of law in any legal system are not necessarily identical in their nature or in the extent of their rights, and their nature depends upon the needs of the community . . .' *Reparations Case* (1949) ICJ Rep 174.

All States possess international legal personality as a result of the principle of sovereign equality. It is often said that they possess 'original' personality. States were considered to be the only subjects of international law during the nineteenth century.

A number of IGOs also possess international legal personality for certain purposes. In addition, individuals have been recognised as having limited forms of international legal personality in certain situations (see below).

The creation of States in international law

International legal personality is a highly valued consequence of the achievement of statehood but how does a political entity become a State?

The test for statehood

> **KEY INSTRUMENT**
>
> **Article 1, Montevideo Convention on the Rights and Duties of States (1933)**
>
> The State as a person of international law should possess the following qualification:
>
> (a) permanent population;
>
> (b) defined territory;
>
> (c) government; and
>
> (d) the capacity to enter into relations with other States.

The Montevideo Convention was a treaty concluded between member States of the Pan-American Union. However, its central provisions have acquired the status of general CIL. Article 1 is indicative of the requirements for the attainment of statehood.

Population

The notion of a permanent population does not indicate that it must be settled. Nomadic populations can count for the purpose of a claim of statehood (see the *Western Sahara Advisory Opinion* (1975) ICJ Rep 12). The important thing is that the population can demonstrate meaningful territorial ties to the political entity in question.

Territory

The requirement that States must have a territorial base is fundamental to the concept of statehood. This was exemplified by Huber J in the *Island of Palmas Case* (1928) 22 AJIL 867 when he said that:

Sovereignty in relations between States signifies independence. Independence in relation to a portion of the globe is the right to exercise therein, to the exclusion of any other State, the functions of a State.

The existence of competing territorial claims by other States or political entities does not undermine claims of statehood (e.g. Israel's boundaries are contested by its neighbours and the Palestinian authorities). No limits have been placed upon the size of a State (either in terms of 'population' or 'territory'). A State can lose substantial parts of its territory (and parts of its population) as a result of a successful act of secession (e.g. the secession of Bangladesh from Pakistan) or the dissolution of a federal State (e.g. USSR/Russia) without the losing its statehood.

▭ REVISION NOTE

You should familiarise yourself with the international law relating to title to territory and self-determination (see Chapter 7).

Government

This criterion refers to the extent to which a political entity is controlled effectively by a governmental authority.

It is helpful to draw a distinction between cases where an entity is making a claim of statehood from situations where an established State is experiencing problems of governance. In general, the government of a new State will need to show that it effectively controls the territory and population in order to achieve statehood. However, an established State may continue to exist despite major instances of civil war, which may have undermined the degree to which the legitimate government controls the State's population and territory. What matters is whether the established government retains the capacity to act on behalf of the State in international affairs.

An established State will not lose its statehood (and thus its international personality) even in the absence of an effective government (e.g. Somalia).

Capacity to enter into international relations with other states

Sovereignty is premised on the notion of independence and equality (see the *Island of Palmas Case* (1928)).

KEY CASE

Austro-German Customs Union Case (1931) PCIJ Series A/B, No. 41

Concerning: whether a customs union would violate international law

Facts

The PCIJ had to decide whether a planned customs union between Germany and Austria would compromise Austria's sovereign independence in contravention of Article 88, Treaty of Saint-Germain (1919) and a 1922 Protocol.

Legal principle

The PCIJ decided that 'independence' as a criterion of statehood was only concerned with a State's formal independence. Accordingly, a State retains its independence if it retains the legal capacity to enter into relations with other States. The fact that a State may be heavily dependent on another State does not undermine its legal independence.

The PCIJ's reasoning on the issue of independence as a criterion of statehood in the *Austro-German Customs Union Case* (1931) has been apparent in more recent times. For example, many East European States were effectively controlled by the USSR during the Cold War but their statehood was never questioned. However, a distinction should be drawn between situations in which a new State is coming into being and where conditions change within established States.

KEY CASE

The Aaland Islands Case (1920) LNOJ Special Sup. No. 3, 3

Concerning: a territorial dispute between Sweden and Finland

Facts

An International Committee of Jurists had to decide on the legality of Finland's break away from the Russian Empire and its subsequent accession to statehood as a matter of international law.

Legal principle

The Committee observed that a constituted State did not exist until a stable political organisation had been created, and until the public authorities had become strong enough to assert themselves without the assistance of the foreign troops. In other words, a new political entity must achieve a degree of *de facto* independence before it can achieve statehood.

How the Montevideo criteria work

There is a link between formal legal independence and the government's ability to control its population and territory effectively in situations where statehood is being claimed. This issue cuts across the Montevideo criteria because it concerns the effectiveness of the government of the aspirant State. In order to be effective the government must exercise a minimum degree of factual independence from other States and be able to control the population and territory of the political entity in question.

Self-determination

The requirement of independence in the *creation* of new States presupposes that a government controls the population and territory of the aspirant State effectively.

However, a lesser degree of effectiveness will be tolerated by international law in certain situations (e.g. the exercise of the right to **self-determination** for colonised peoples). This right may remedy particular difficulties that an aspirant State would have had in satisfying the Montevideo criteria.

KEY CASE

Congo's Independence (1960)

Concerning: the principle of self-determination

Facts

Congo was a Belgian colony. The prospect of decolonisation led to internal conflict, secessionist activity and the intervention of Belgian military forces to maintain order. Congo became a State in 1960. However, it clearly did not satisfy the Montevideo criteria for the creation of States in international law.

Legal principle

International law recognises that all colonial peoples possess the right of self-determination. As a result, the newly established State of Congo was widely recognised as a State by other States and it was admitted to the UN despite the fact that the effectiveness of the new Congolese government was disrupted. In the circumstances, the right to self-determination overcame Congo's inability to satisfy the Montevideo criteria at the moment of independence.

✎ EXAM TIP

It is important to remember that, traditionally, international law was not concerned with the internal affairs of sovereign States. States were considered to be free to choose their own domestic institutional arrangements (e.g. see Art. 2(7) UN Charter). Consequently, under established international law, States are not bound to adopt democratic governmental practices. Nevertheless, you should consider the extent to which democratic practices might strengthen a claim of statehood.

Statehood and UN membership

UN membership creates a presumption in favour of statehood. It may confirm that an aspirant State has been accepted as a State by the international community of States. However, UN membership is not constitutive of statehood. States have existed without being UN members (e.g. Switzerland did not become a full UN member until 2002).

Article 4, UN Charter (1945)

(1) UN membership is open to all other peace-loving states which accept the obligations contained in the present Charter and, in the judgment of the Organization, are able and willing to carry out these obligations.

(2) The admission of any such state to membership in the United Nations will be effected by a decision of the General Assembly upon the recommendation of the Security Council.

■ Recognition of States in international law

States may choose to recognise a claim of statehood made by a political entity. Recognition is one of the ways by which States address the issue of the creation of States in international law. International law lacks a centralised authority that has the power to determine whether a State has satisfied the test of statehood. One view is that States either grant or withhold recognition of a putative State on their own behalf and on behalf of the international community.

❗ Don't be tempted to . . .

Don't confuse the topic of recognition of States with recognition of governments. While these areas share certain concepts they are different in important respects.

KEY DEFINITION: The purpose of recognition

'The purpose of recognition is to endow the new entity with capacity vis-à-vis the recognising State, to be a bearer of rights and duties under international law and participate in international relations on the footing of international law.' Schwarzenberger (1976).

Figure 4.1
Test for statehood

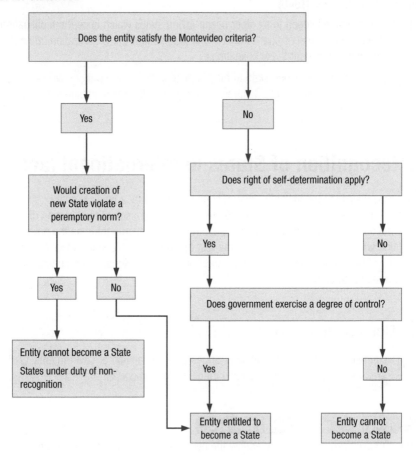

Non-recognition: supervening illegality

International law will *not* endorse claims of statehood that are made by political entities – even where they are effective – where this would result in the violation of peremptory norms (e.g. the right to self-determination; the prohibition on the use of force; or the prohibition on racial discrimination).

KEY CASE

Manchukuo (1931–1933)

Concerning: the purpose of non-recognition

Facts

Japan invaded and annexed the northern Chinese province of Manchuria in 1931. It claimed to have established the new State of Manchukuo.

Legal principle

Japan controlled the population and territory of Manchuria effectively. However, the annexation of Manchuria was conducted in violation of the prohibition on the use of force contained in the Kellogg–Briand Pact (1928). A League of Nations Report concluded that the 'government of Manchukuo' lacked independence and authority. States refused to recognise Manchukuo as a State.

☐ REVISION NOTE

The provisions of the Kellogg–Briand Pact (1928) concerning the prohibition on use of force have been superseded by Article 2(4) of the UN Charter. (See Chapter 10.)

KEY CASE

Southern Rhodesia (1965)

Concerning: the non-recognition of Southern Rhodesia's declaration of independence

Facts

Southern Rhodesia was a British colony. In 1965, the white regime in charge of the colonial government made a unilateral declaration of independence (a claim of statehood). This step was viewed as an attempt to deny the colonised people the right of self-determination and to perpetuate a system based on racial discrimination.

Legal principle

UNSC in SC Resolution 216 (1965) urged 'all States not to recognise this illegal racist minority regime'. States refused to recognise Southern Rhodesia as a State.

Cases of recognition

Recognition can remedy weaknesses in a claim to statehood. As noted above, the right of self-determination may strengthen a claim to statehood. States may endorse such a claim by deciding to recognise the political entity.

Make your answer stand out

Many States have shown their willingness to recognise the existence of a Palestinian State even though the Palestinian authorities do not currently control the population and territory in question. It is widely acknowledged the Palestinian 'people' possess the right of self-determination in international law. You should explore the reasons why this right has not influenced the 'Palestinian Question' significantly. Further, you should reflect upon the problematic nature of self-determination conflicts. See the *Advisory Opinion concerning the Legal Consequences of the Construction of a Wall in the Occupied Palestinian Territories* (2004) ICJ Rep 136 and Crawford (2006).

KEY CASE

Bosnia-Herzegovina (1991–1995)

Concerning: the recognition of the State of Bosnia-Herzegovina

Facts

Bosnia-Herzegovina sought to be recognised as a State by the EC despite the fact that Bosnian Serb paramilitaries controlled significant parts of its territory at that time (consequently, it did not have a sufficient degree of independence to satisfy the Montevideo criteria).

Legal principle

A substantial degree of international administration was introduced in Bosnia-Herzegovina under the Dayton Peace Agreement (1995) which exercised specific governmental functions and thus enabled the new State to be created (via UN SC Res.1031(1995)).

KEY CASE

Kosovo's Declaration of Independence (2008)

Concerning: the recognition of the State of Kosovo

Facts

The Yugoslav province of Kosovo was administered by the UN Mission in Kosovo (UNMIK) pursuant to UNSCR 1244 (1999). In 2008, the Kosovo parliament made a declaration of independence. The aspirant State did not have a sufficient degree of independence in order to satisfy the Montevideo criteria and its claim contradicted the notional sovereignty held in respect of the territory by Serbia/Yugoslavia which had been acknowledged in UN SC Res. 1244 (1999)).

Legal principle

Many States have recognised Kosovo (including the US and the UK). However, Russia and China have refused to recognise it. Some international lawyers have claimed that the people of Kosovo possess the right of self-determination and the declaration of independence constituted an exercise of it.

 Make your answer stand out

States which have recognised Kosovo have preferred not to express the legal basis for their decision. Is Kosovo a case of self-determination? Do you think that States are worried about the potential for the right of self-determination to be used as a means of dissolving federal States? Does the case of Kosovo demonstrate the overt political nature of recognition? Kosovo is not a UN member. Russia would use its veto in the UNSC if Kosovo made an application for admission. Can it be a State without this status? See Weller (2008).

Recognition theories

Declaratory theory

KEY DEFINITION: Declaratory theory of recognition

'[T]he existence or disappearance of the State is a question of fact . . . the effects of recognition are purely declaratory' – Opinion No. 1, EC Arbitration Commission on Yugoslavia (1991) 31 ILM 1494.S

KEY INSTRUMENT

Montevideo Convention (1933)

Article 3: 'The political existence of the State is independent of recognition by other States.'

Article 6: 'The recognition of a State merely signifies that the State which recognizes it accepts the personality of the other with all the rights and duties determined by international law words.'

Despite the above provisions of the Montevideo Convention (1933), recognition does confirm that a political entity, which claims to be a State, has attained that status.

The problem with the declaratory theory is that it ignores the fact that the value of statehood flows from its connection with international legal personality. A new State is able to participate with established States in the inter-State system. If existing States refuse to deal with it, the fact that the State exists will have very little significance. An unrecognised State will not be able to enter into multilateral treaties, be admitted to the UN, or establish diplomatic missions.

Constitutive theory of recognition

KEY DEFINITION: Constitutive theory of recognition

It is the act of recognition by other States that creates the new State by endowing it with legal existence. A new State is created by the will of existing States.

The **constitutive theory of recognition** is tainted by its association with the colonialism of the late nineteenth century when admission to the 'Family of Nations' was controlled by the colonial powers and through which they denied that political entities could be States unless they could meet European standards of 'civilisation'. The Montevideo Convention sought to replace the constitutive view with the declarative one by stressing the importance of effectiveness rather than the judgement of existing States.

The current approach

Modern international law favours a modified declaratory theory of recognition. It appreciates that established States do exert a degree of influence when political entities are seeking to become States, if those aspirant States have difficulty in satisfying the Montevideo criteria. This will be especially important in cases of secession and State dissolution. Consequently, recognition performs an evidential function in borderline cases.

KEY CASE

EC Guidelines on the Recognition of New States in Eastern Europe and USSR (1991) 31 ILM 1499–1500

Concerning: the recognition of new States in Eastern Europe and USSR

Facts

The EC adopted a common recognition policy regarding the former Soviet republics that wished to accede to statehood. The Guidelines were also applied to the former Yugoslav republics on the dissolution of Yugoslavia.

Legal principle

The Guidelines indicated that the following requirements must be satisfied for recognition to be accorded to a new State:

- respect for the rule of law, democracy and human rights;
- acceptance of disarmament/nuclear proliferation commitments;
- guarantees for ethnic minorities;
- acceptance of the peaceful resolution of disputes;
- commitment to renounce territorial claims against neighbouring States.

Relationship between statehood and recognition

Recognition is not a criterion for statehood. However, the EC Guidelines appear to have added to the Montevideo criteria for the creation of new States. This has led some international lawyers to argue that new States must be democratic and observe human rights. Nevertheless, in practice, the additional criteria have not been treated as if they are binding as a matter of international law. Instead they illustrate the political nature of the act of recognition.

It is important to draw a distinction between the creation of a new State and the willingness of established States to recognise a new State. Recognition only confirms that a political entity has become a State. However, it is significant when that entity has difficulty in satisfying the Montevideo criteria (e.g. the people of a particular region are trying to secede from a State with the aim of creating a new State pursuant to the right of self-determination).

✎ EXAM TIP

Many existing States would not satisfy the EC Guidelines. Does this suggest that they are not essential requirements for the creation of States in international law? If established States that are not democratic, do not observe human rights, and are not committed to the rule of law sought to achieve statehood today would they be recognised as States? Understanding the legal and political aspects inherent within recognition will help you to enhance your understanding of this topic.

■ International Governmental Organisations (IGOs)

During the twentieth century, the view that only States possessed international legal personality was challenged by the creation of IGOs that exercised a degree of independence from the States that had created them. The founding of the UN accelerated this development considerably. There are now some 200 IGOs and many of them enjoy a degree of international personality.

IGOs have been given certain tasks and therefore typically they are given a degree of functional autonomy so that they discharge their responsibilities. However, the question of whether IGOs were endowed with international legal personality was not fully appreciated when the UN was founded.

KEY CASE

Reparations Advisory Opinion (1949) ICJ Rep 174

Concerning: whether the UN had the legal capacity to claim reparation for injuries suffered in its service

Facts

Two members of the UN staff were killed in a part of Jerusalem that was controlled by the State of Israel. The UN sought compensation from Israel. The ICJ had to decide whether the UN had international legal personality needed in order to make such a claim.

Legal principle

The ICJ held that the UN did have legal personality for this and other purposes:

'The [UN] was intended to exercise and enjoy, and is in fact exercising and enjoying, functions and rights which can be explained on the basis of the possession of a large measure of international personality . . .'

IGOs may have their international legal personality expressly conferred upon them in their constituent treaty. However, in the *Reparations Case* (1949), the ICJ noted that international legal personality could also be conferred by implication:

Under international law, the [UN] must be deemed to have those powers which . . . are conferred upon it by necessary implication as being essential to the performance of its duties.

In the absence of express provision, whether an IGO has international legal personality depends on its purpose and function.

UN

The UN has *full* international legal personality. It has:

- the capacity to make legal claims;
- the authority to enter into international treaties and other agreements;
- law-making powers within its sphere of competence (e.g. UNSC resolutions constitute binding international law – see Article 25, UN Charter).

Moreover, the UN has objective legal personality. In the ICJ's view:

> The vast majority of the members of the international community, had the power, in conformity with international law, to bring into being an entity possessing *objective* international personality . . . (*Reparations Case* (1949))

Two observations can be made in relation to this passage:

- The UN possesses *derivative* personality (the same is true for other IGOs that possess international legal personality). The States that participated in the creation of an IGO which has been endowed with international legal personality have given it its personality (in contrast, States possess original personality).
- The UN has the capacity to create legal obligations for all States (obligations *erga omnes*), even States that did not participate in its creation (or States that were subsequently admitted to the UN). Consequently, it has the power to create international law that is binding upon States irrespective of their consent.

EXAM TIP

Given that nearly all States are now UN members the *erga omnes* nature of the UN may seem to be an academic point. However, it does demonstrate the limits of the consent model of international law and therefore it challenges the basis of international legal obligation discussed in Chapter 1. This point allows you to reflect generally on the nature of international law and to advance wider arguments in the context of a discussion about international legal personality.

- Most IGOs only possess *subjective* (or qualified) international legal personality. Consequently they only have legal personality vis-à-vis their member States. An IGO with qualified personality can only create international law for those States which are parties to its constituent treaty. For example, the International Tin Council only had the legal authority to regulate matters within its sphere of competence in relation to its member States (see *Maclaine Watson* v *DTI* (1990) discussed in Chapter 5).

EU

The European Union has the authority to create law for its member States (and for their inhabitants). However, it cannot create law for third States.

Article 281 of the EC Treaty (1957) expressly recognised that the European *Community* possessed 'legal personality'. Case 22/70 *Commission* v *Council* [1971] ECR 263 interpreted this as international legal personality.

Article 47 of the Treaty of the European Union (as amended by the Treaty of Lisbon 2007) recognised that the EU has international legal personality. The EU can:

- conclude treaties/agreements with third States and other IGOs;
- bring international legal claims against third States and against its own member States;
- create law for its member States (and individuals within those States) via Regulations, Treaty Articles and Directives.

Individuals

The traditional position

International law is an inter-State legal system and so States act on behalf of their nationals. Consequently, it was thought that individuals did not possess *direct* international legal rights and obligations – they did not have international legal personality. However, the traditional position is no longer accurate.

Individual obligations

It has been recognised that individuals have duties as a matter of international law. So far these obligations have been restricted to the criminal sphere. The notion of individual criminal responsibility was first applied by the International Military Tribunal at Nuremberg in 1946 in connection with atrocities committed by the Nazi regime during the Second World War. This Tribunal was authorised to adjudicate crimes against humanity and war crimes.

The concept of individual criminal responsibility was developed and applied by the UN Security Council on an ad hoc basis when it established the International Criminal Tribunal for Rwanda and the International Criminal Tribunal for Yugoslavia. Individual criminal responsibility has become more generally applicable with the setting up of the ICC via Article 25, Rome Statute (1998). (See Chapter 1.)

Figure 4.2
International legal personality (ILP) of IGOs

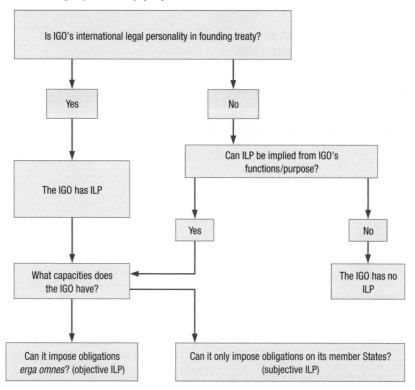

Individual rights

It is now accepted that individuals have rights at the level of international law. However, these rights are dependent on particular States having given their consent to the rights in question. For example, an individual cannot be said to have a particular right contained in a multilateral treaty unless his or her State has ratified that treaty. So individuals may have *indirect* international legal rights. Further, whether that right can be enforced depends on the institutional machinery and procedures which accompany the right in question.

For example, Article 36(1), Vienna Convention on Consular Relations (1963) confers an individual right of consular access upon nationals of those States which have ratified the Convention (this was confirmed by the ICJ in the *La Grand Case* (2001) (see Chapter 8). However, the ICJ only has jurisdiction to consider a complaint if the State in question ratified the optional protocol to the 1963 Convention.

Individuals have the right to make legal claims in certain regional legal systems, including:

- to the European Court of Human Rights in respect of the European Convention on Human Rights (1950) (Art. 34);
- to the Inter-American Court on Human Rights in respect of the Inter-American Convention on Human Rights (1969).

■ Putting it all together

Answer guidelines

See the problem question at the start of the chapter.

Approaching the question

This question involves the following areas:

- creation of States in international law;
- scope of the right of self-determination;
- role of recognition in the creation of States.

Important points to include

- For Beta to achieve statehood it must be able to satisfy the Montevideo criteria:
  - ☐ To what extent does the Betan government control its territory effectively?
  - ☐ Is Arcadia's control of Betan territory significant?
  - ☐ Does the prospect of UN membership and evidence of UN support suggest that the Betan government has the capacity to enter into international relations?
- The right of self-determination can relax some of the rules concerning the creation of States:
  - ☐ Do the Betan people possess the right of self-determination?
  - ☐ Does this right justify secession (e.g. Kosovo)? (See Chapter 7.)
- Recognition can provide valuable evidence in support of a claim to statehood in difficult cases:
  - ☐ What are the recognition theories and how do they apply in this scenario?
  - ☐ Is it significant that Beta has been recognised by 50 States?

☐ What is the impact of UN membership?

☐ Does it matter that Arcadia has a permanent seat on the UN Security Council? See Article 4 UN Charter.

 Make your answer stand out

■ Provide detailed analysis of the scope of self-determination and examples of its application.

■ Provide contextual analysis of whether Beta could meet the criteria set out in the EC Guidelines (1991).

■ Examine relevant cases/examples to show how statehood, self-determination and recognition work together in practice.

READ TO IMPRESS

Brownlie, I. (1982) 'Recognition in Theory and Practice', 53 *BYIL* 197.

Craven, M. (1995) 'The European Community Arbitration Commission on Yugoslavia', *BYIL* 66, 333.

Crawford, J. R. (2006) *The Creation of States in International Law*, 2nd edn. Oxford University Press.

Schwarzenberger, G. (1976) *International Law*. Sweet & Maxwell.

Weller, M. (2008) *Contested Statehood: Kosovo's Struggle for Independence*. Oxford University Press.

www.pearsoned.co.uk/lawexpress

 Go online to access more revision support including quizzes to test your knowledge, sample questions with answer guidelines, podcasts you can download, and more!

International law
and national law

5

Revision checklist

Essential points you should know:

☐ Theories about the relationship between international law and national law

☐ Doctrines concerning the application of international law within national legal systems

☐ International views about the reception of international law into national law

☐ Status and effect of national legal rules within international litigation

■ Topic map

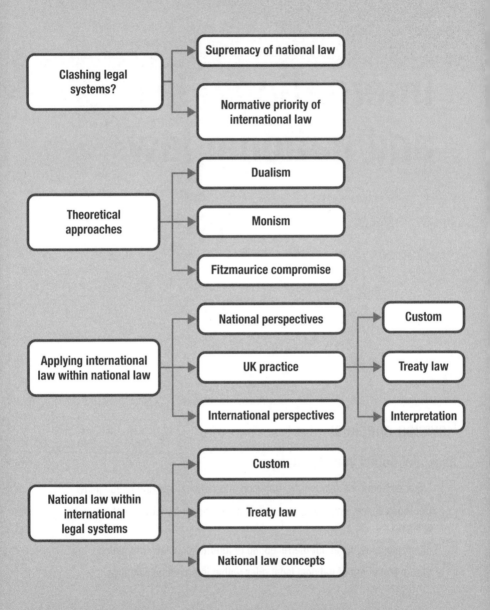

A printable version of this topic map is available from **www.pearsoned.co.uk/lawexpress**

■ Introduction

Are national legal systems subordinate to international law or is it the other way around? Are national courts bound to apply international legal rules? Does national legislation have to comply with international law? What is the status and effect of national legal rules in disputes before international courts? International law developed as an inter-State legal system concerned with a narrow range of legal issues. This restrictive approach remains consistent with State sovereignty and the belief that international law is created by State consent. However, international law is increasingly concerned with matters that would have been considered to be within the exclusive jurisdiction of States in earlier times (e.g. the protection of human rights). Consequently, the extent to which international legal rights/obligations can be enforced within national legal systems has become a pressing concern.

ASSESSMENT ADVICE

Essay questions

Essay questions often concern the obstacles that restrict the application of international law in national legal systems. To answer such questions you will need to have a good understanding of the relevant theories, doctrines and cases. You should appreciate the effect that different sources have on the issue of reception of international law into national law.

Problem questions

Problem questions tend to focus on situations where international law and national law are in conflict. It is important that you organise your answer effectively: identify the critical issues; tackle distinct issues separately; and apply the appropriate doctrines and rules with reference to legal authority. You should also note that other topics may also be relevant to your answer (e.g. jurisdiction and sources).

■ Sample question

Could you answer this question? Below is a typical problem question that could arise on this topic. Guidelines on answering the question are included at the end of this chapter, whilst a sample essay question and guidance on tackling it can be found on the companion website.

The (fictitious) Territorial Sea (Jurisdiction) Act 1962 provides that the UK is entitled to exercise full jurisdiction up to 15 miles from its coastline. In 2010, two ships, *The Bounty* and *The Endeavour*, collide at a point 13 miles from the UK's coast. The collision was caused by the negligence of *The Endeavour*'s Brazilian captain, Miguel Sanchez, and resulted in the death of two crew members of *The Bounty*. *The Bounty* was registered in Greece and its crew were all Greek nationals. *The Endeavour* was registered in Brazil and its crew were Brazilian nationals. The UK authorities prosecuted Sanchez for manslaughter under UK law. Under a rule of customary international law, States are only entitled to claim full jurisdiction over maritime areas that are not more than 12 miles from their coasts. Brazil formally protested that the collision occurred on the High Seas and that the UK had no jurisdiction to prosecute Sanchez. The UK government ignored the protest. Sanchez was subsequently convicted for the crime of manslaughter in the UK courts. Brazil instituted legal proceedings before the ICJ against the UK alleging that the UK had violated international law. Advise the UK government as to the legality of its actions under international law.

Clashing legal systems?

Supremacy of national law

State sovereignty is the core principle of international law: States retained considerable freedom of action in areas which remain unregulated by international law (the *Lotus* principle (see Chapter 1)).

- International law cannot 'intervene in matters which are essentially within the domestic jurisdiction' of any State (Art. 2(7), UN Charter).

- International law is created by State consent and States are not bound by international legal rules to which they have not assented (see Chapter 2).

- The authority of State officials to make national laws arises from the exercise of the right to national self-determination (see Chapter 7).

- Governments consent to the creation of international law. However, typically national laws can only be made by the national legislature and so this difference in law-making authority has constitutional implications (see below).

Normative priority of international law

- A State's sovereignty is guaranteed by international law on behalf of the international society of States – it is not an absolute concept (see Chapter 1).

- International law recognises certain fundamental universal rights/obligations that bind all States (e.g. peremptory norms (see Chapter 2)).

- Arguably, international law exists to serve a higher purpose – the achievement of respect for human dignity. This purpose justifies international regulation of matters that fall within the domestic jurisdiction of States and national legal systems should facilitate this overriding moral imperative.

- States have consented to the creation of international law. Their constitutional arrangements should not act as a barrier to the implementation of international legal rights/obligations (see Chapter 3).

- States may bear international responsibility when international legal rights/obligations are not implemented in national law (see Chapter 8).

□ REVISION NOTE

The relationship between international law and national law raises fundamental issues about the nature and purpose of international law. It is therefore very important to develop a holistic understanding of international law in order to produce good answers on this topic.

■ Theoretical approaches

Dualism

KEY DEFINITION: Dualism

International law and national law constitute entirely separate legal systems.

- An international legal rule has no legal validity within a national legal system.

- For an international legal rule to acquire legal validity in national law it must be turned into a national legal rule (either via national legislation or by judicial decision) before it can have legal effect.

- **Dualism** guards against the risk of national laws being determined by institutions beyond the State by ensuring that the legislature and the courts retain the constitutional authority to decide the content of national law.

- Dualism is widely thought to endorse positivism. It promotes the importance of the role of State consent and the concept of State sovereignty in the creation and operation of international law.

Monism

KEY DEFINITION: Monism

International law and national law are components of a single legal system.

- International law should be directly effective within national law for ethical reasons. Monists tend to embrace universalism/the natural law tradition. Consequently, **monism** is very persuasive at an ideological level:
  - individuals are the ultimate subjects of both international and national legal subsystems thereby justifying the creation and enforcement of universal human rights;
  - the development of global forms of law to tackle global problems (e.g. the drive for multilateral treaties regarding widespread environmental risks).
- The monist outlook has been strengthened by the development of universal/fundamental rights/obligations during the UN era (see Chapter 1).

EXAM TIP

It is worthwhile considering the extent to which monism and dualism are actually followed in State practice. States which have adopted a dualist approach include the UK and the US. Greece, Netherlands and Spain have adopted a (qualified) monist approach. See Denza (2010).

The 'Fitzmaurice compromise'

The relationship between international law and national legal systems should be considered from the perspective of conflicting legal obligations that exist at different legal levels. If a State enacts domestic legislation that conflicts with a binding international legal obligation it will incur international responsibility (and thus liability) on the international plane for violating international law. However, the offending national legislation will still be valid under national law.

EXAM TIP

You should note that the prospect of a claim of international responsibility arguably provides an incentive for States to make sure that their national laws conform to international legal standards (thus achieving a practical harmony between international law and national law). You should also revise the topic of State responsibility (Chapter 8) alongside this chapter.

■ Applying international law within national legal systems

International law increasingly seeks to regulate issues that fall within States' domestic jurisdiction (e.g. human rights, criminal law and environmental law). Moreover, these legal regimes are becoming more comprehensive in scope and the institutional apparatus which supports them is becoming sophisticated. Against this changing background, how do the international legal system and national legal systems coordinate their respective legal rights and obligations?

National perspectives

States have adopted different approaches to the way in which international law is received into their national legal systems. However, two doctrines can be identified: **incorporation** and **transformation**.

KEY DEFINITION: Incorporation

International law is *automatically* part of national law. In principle, a national court is bound to apply international legal rules where they are relevant to a case before it.

KEY DEFINITION: Transformation

International law only becomes part of national law if something is done to transform it into national law (either by enacting national legislation which gives effect to an international legal rule in national law or the decision of the national courts).

! Don't be tempted to . . .

Many States have adopted the doctrine of incorporation in relation to the reception of CIL rules into national law while following the doctrine of transformation regarding the reception of treaty law. Do not suggest that States adhere to one or other doctrine in general.

■ UK practice

CIL

UK law seems to follow the doctrine of incorporation in respect of CIL rules.

KEY CASE

R v *Keyn* (1876–7) LR 2 Ex D 63

Concerning: the exercise of criminal jurisdiction beyond British territorial waters

Facts

Two ships, the *Franconia* (German) and the *Strathclyde* (British), collided at a point less than three miles from the UK's coast. A passenger on the *Strathclyde* died as a result. The *Franconia*'s captain was prosecuted for manslaughter in the UK courts. Did the collision occur within the UK's jurisdiction?

Legal principle

It was argued that a CIL rule existed which entitled States to exercise jurisdiction up to a point of three miles from their coastlines. However, the court decided that, because Parliament had not enacted legislation providing for such jurisdiction as a matter of UK law, it had no jurisdiction over the accused. The case endorses the doctrine of incorporation.

KEY CASE

Mortensen v *Peters* (1906) 14 SLT 227

Concerning: the exercise of criminal jurisdiction beyond British territorial waters

Facts

The Scottish Fishery Board issued delegated legislation under a statute that made it an offence to engage in certain types of fishing. A Danish captain of a Norwegian ship contravened the legislation. He was tried and convicted for this offence in a UK court. However, he had been fishing beyond the three-mile territorial limit recognised by CIL.

Legal principle

The court decided that, even though the vessel in question was more than three miles from the coast, the statute purported to exercise jurisdiction over it and, by necessary implication, the court was bound to apply the terms of the statute.

KEY CASE

Trendtex Trading v *Central Bank of Nigeria* [1977] QB 529

Concerning: a claim of State immunity for the debts of the government body
Legal issue: the relationship between CIL and UK law in respect of claims of State
immunity in civil matters

Facts

Under an agreement Trendtex sold cement to the Nigerian government to be used in the construction of public buildings. The government instructed its central bank not to pay for the cement. Trendtex sued the bank in the UK courts. The bank made a claim of absolute State immunity and that, as a result, the UK courts had no jurisdiction over the dispute.

Legal principle

The court held that the CIL rule concerning absolute State immunity had been replaced by a new CIL rule of restrictive State immunity in situations where a State had engaged in a commercial activity. This new CIL rule had become part of UK law automatically via the doctrine of incorporation.

KEY CASE

R v *Margaret Jones and Others* [2007] 1 AC 136

Concerning: the availability of CIL as a defence to national criminal charges

Facts

The defendants were prosecuted in the UK courts for causing criminal damage to UK and US military bases. They argued that they were trying to prevent the CIL crime of aggression – the invasion of Iraq. They claimed, under the doctrine of incorporation, this crime was automatically part of UK law and it was a valid defence to the charges against them.

Legal principle

HL accepted that the crime of aggression was a CIL rule. However, it doubted whether CIL rules can become part of UK law automatically. This can only happen when it is permitted by the constitution. The courts are no longer able to introduce new criminal offences into UK law – this is a matter for Parliament acting through statute. Consequently, legislation was required to transform this CIL crime into domestic law. Without such legislation it was not part of UK law and thus could not be a valid defence to the charges of criminal damage.

Make your answer stand out

You should consider the constitutional background to the above cases. The UK government acts for the UK in international affairs. However, it does not have the constitutional authority to make UK law. If the UK courts adopt the view that CIL rules are part of UK law automatically, in effect, the government could make UK law (acting in association with other States). Is this acceptable from a constitutional law point of view? See Sales and Clement (2008).

The UK courts increasingly seem to insist that CIL rules should be transformed into UK law by statute. However, CIL rules can still become UK law via the doctrine of incorporation in appropriate non-criminal cases. See *Kuwait Airways* v *Iraqi Airways (Nos. 4 and 5)* [2002] 2 AC 883.

Treaty law

Parliamentary sovereignty is the UK constitution's most important legal principle. A treaty can only become UK law if it has been transformed by an Act of Parliament.

KEY CASE

The Parlement Belge (1879–80) LR 5 PD 197

Concerning: claim of State immunity in response to a civil claim
Legal issue: a treaty must be transformed into national law by statute if it is to be justiciable in the UK courts

Facts

The Parlement Belge was a ship owned by the Belgian king. It collided with an English boat which sustained damage as a result. The owner sued the Belgian king in the UK courts. A claim of sovereign immunity was made (relying upon a treaty concluded between the UK and Belgian governments). If the immunity claim were successful the court would have no jurisdiction to decide the case.

Legal principle

At first instance, the judge decided that the claim amounted to 'a use of the treaty making prerogative of the Crown which I believe to be without precedence and in principle contrary to the laws of the constitution'. Consequently, the judge decided that the court had jurisdiction to decide the case. This decision was reversed by the Court of Appeal (it decided that sovereign immunity was established in CIL (see Chapter 6)).

KEY CASE

Maclaine Watson v *DTI* [1990] 2 AC 418

Concerning: State liability for the debts of an IGO

Facts

The International Tin Council (ITC) was an IGO created by treaty. It was wound up and its creditors brought claims against the UK government on the ground that the ITC's member States were liable for its debts. The treaty had not been incorporated into UK law by statute.

Legal principle

HL decided that a treaty that had not been transformed into UK law by statute could not form the basis of litigation in the UK courts.

Parliament had no constitutional role in the negotiation and conclusion of treaties. The constitutional practice – the Ponsonby rule – was that a signed treaty is laid before Parliament for a period of 21 days, giving it the opportunity to debate the treaty before it was ratified. The Constitutional Reform and Governance Act 2010 has developed the Ponsonby rule and put it on a statutory footing.

✎ EXAM TIP

Parliament does not approve the treaties made by the UK government. You could contrast this position with the approach adopted by other States. For example, Article 2, US Constitution provides that the US President can only ratify treaties that have been approved by at least two-thirds of the Senate. See Denza (2010).

 Make your answer stand out

What is the basis for the distinction between CIL and treaty law regarding the reception of international law into UK law? The orthodox view holds that a treaty must be transformed into domestic law by statute because the government cannot create UK law indirectly. However, CIL is also made by the government (acting on behalf of the UK) without parliamentary involvement. Why can CIL become part of UK law automatically (in appropriate cases) but not treaty law? Is this source-based approach flawed?

The Human Rights Act (HRA) 1998

The doctrines of incorporation and transformation *cannot* account for the operation of the Human Rights Act (HRA) 1998. The UK government ratified the European Convention on Human Rights (ECHR) in 1951 but it was not transformed into UK law by statute so the Convention was not part of UK law. Consequently, Convention rights could not be directly enforced in the English courts (see *R* v *Secretary of State for the Home Department ex parte Brind* (1991) below).

The HRA gave effect to Convention rights in the UK without transforming the Convention into UK law. Thus, while Convention rights are part of UK law, the Convention itself is not directly enforceable in UK courts. The Convention and the jurisprudence of the European Court of Human Rights (ECtHR) are rendered effective (indirectly) through interpretation of the HRA provisions by the UK courts.

KEY INSTRUMENT

Section 3(1), HRA

'So far as it is possible to do so, primary legislation and subordinate legislation must be read and given effect in a way which is compatible with the Convention Rights.'

The HRA requires the UK courts to construe UK legislation so that it is consistent with Convention rights (see *Ghaidan* v *Godin-Mendoza* (2004)). Under section 6 HRA, all public authorities are subject to the Convention obligations identified in the Act.

The doctrines of incorporation and transformation *cannot* explain instances where treaty provisions have been applied by the UK courts where they have not been transformed by statute:

- *R (Al-Jedda)* v *Secretary of State for Defence* [2008] 1 AC 332, where the HL held that a UN Security Council resolution could override the HRA.

- *A* v *Secretary of State for the Home Department (No. 2)* [2006] AC 221, where the HL held that the common law reflected Article 14, Torture Convention (1984) (regarding the inadmissibility of evidence obtained as a result of torture) even though this treaty provision had not been enacted into UK law. HL viewed the prohibition on torture as a peremptory norm that gave rise to obligations *erga omnes* (see Chapter 2).

 Make your answer stand out

You should consider whether the above examples are indicative of a shift away from consideration of the source of the international legal obligations/rights (whether they arise in CIL or from treaty law) to an approach determined by the subject matter of the dispute. See Capps (2007).

Interpretation

In UK law, there is a presumption that Parliament intends to legislate in a way that is consistent with the UK's international legal obligations. The courts seek to interpret UK law in a way that does not conflict with international law, where this is possible. However, this is only a rule of interpretation. If a statute clearly contradicts international law then the courts are bound to give effect to the will of Parliament regardless of whether State responsibility under international law is engaged (see Chapter 8).

KEY CASE

***R v Secretary of State for the Home Department, ex parte Brind* [1991] 1 AC 696**

Concerning: whether the ECHR was justiciable in UK courts

Facts

The Home Secretary was authorised, by statute, to require broadcasters to refrain from transmitting words spoken by representatives of certain proscribed terrorist organisations in Northern Ireland. The applicants claimed that the Secretary of State's directives were unlawful because they breached Article 10, ECHR (the right to freedom of expression).

Legal principle

The provisions of a treaty to which the UK government is a party cannot trump the clearly expressed terms of a statute.

Figure 5.1

Reception of international law into national law (UK)

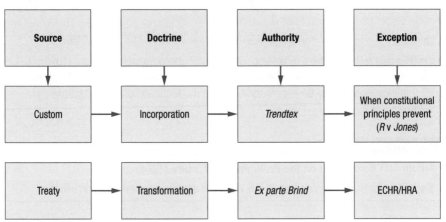

91

✎ EXAM TIP

It is worth making the effort to find out the doctrinal approaches adopted by other national legal systems within this context. This information can be compared and contrasted with the various practices adopted by the UK. Good examples include the US, the Netherlands and Greece. See Denza (2010).

International perspectives

International institutions try to ensure that the international law is effective. The international legal system's institutional weaknesses (see Chapter 1) mean that it relies upon States to render international law effective through their national legal systems. If States could avoid their international legal obligations easily then international law would remain a very weak form of law. Unsurprisingly, international courts have tried to ensure that applicable international legal rules cannot be easily set aside by national law.

Must national legislation comply with international law? A State may be held to be responsible if:

■ its domestic law allows for the undertaking of actions (or omissions) that violate international law; and

■ acts are done (or not done) which breach international law; and

■ those acts or omissions are attributable to the State.

📖 REVISION NOTE

When revising this topic you should refer to the rules concerning State responsibility. (See Chapter 8.)

The duty to enact national legislation is typically included within multilateral treaties.

According to the PCIJ in the *Exchange of Greek and Turkish Populations Case* (1925): 'a State which has contracted valid international obligations is bound to make in its legislation such modifications as may be necessary to ensure the fulfilment of the obligations undertaken' (at 20).

KEY INSTRUMENT

Article 4(1) Convention on the Prohibition of Torture (1984)

'Each State Party shall ensure that all acts of torture are offences under its criminal law . . .'

This 'prevention rather than cure' approach tries to ensure that *fundamental* international rights/obligations are rendered effective within national legal systems. It seeks to coordinate international and national legal rights and obligations so as to give effect to universally held values (see *Furundzija* (1998) 121 ILR 213). However, there is no duty to enact national legislation that complies with international law other than in areas where peremptory norms and binding treaty obligations exist to that effect.

◾ National law in the international legal system

CIL

States cannot invoke national legal rules to avoid their international legal obligations and thus avoid State responsibility for actions that violate international law.

> **KEY CASE**
>
> *The Alabama Arbitration* (1872) Moore 1 Int Arb 495
>
> *Concerning: State responsibility where national law is inconsistent with international legal obligations*
>
> **Facts**
>
> The US brought a claim against the UK for damage sustained against Union ships during the American Civil War by a number of Confederate war ships that were built in the UK (despite the UK government's declaration of neutrality concerning the Civil War). These ships were not fitted as war ships in the UK. However, it was generally known that they would be subsequently fitted with guns, etc. and that they would be used in that war.
>
> **Legal principle**
>
> The Arbitration Panel decided in favour of the US government: 'a neutral government must take care . . . that its municipal law shall prohibit acts contravening neutrality'.

This position was reinforced by the PCIJ in the *Polish Nationals in Danzig Case* (1932) when it served that: 'a State cannot adduce as against another State its own constitution with a view to evading obligations incumbent upon it under international law or treaties in force.'

Treaty law

> **KEY INSTRUMENT**
>
> **Article 27 VCLT (1969)**
>
> 'A party may not invoke the provisions of its internal law as justification for its failure to perform a treaty.'

This approach has been reinforced by the ICJ in the *La Grand Case* (2001) and the *Avena Case* (2004), which both concerned the US's failure to comply with its obligations under the Vienna Convention on Consular Relations (1963) as a result of its national law provisions. (See Chapter 9.)

KEY INSTRUMENT

Article 46(1) VCLT (1969)

'A State may not invoke the fact that its consent to be bound by a treaty has been expressed in violation of a provision of its internal law regarding competence to conclude treaties as invalidating its consent.'

KEY CASE

Cameroon v *Nigeria* (2002) ICJ Rep 303

Concerning: a territorial/maritime boundary dispute
Legal issue: a State cannot invoke the provisions of its national law to avoid international legal obligations

Facts

Nigeria claimed that a bilateral treaty between the two States was invalid because even though it had been signed by Nigeria's Head of State, it had not been ratified by the legislature.

Legal principle

A Head of State has the authority to conclude a treaty on behalf of his or her State (under Art. 7(2) VCLT). Consequently, international legal obligations cannot be avoided by reference to that State's domestic law (see Art. 46(1) VCLT).

📖 **REVISION NOTE**

It is useful to revise treaty law alongside the present topic (Chapter 3).

The use of national law concepts by international courts

International courts frequently use national law principles via Article 38(1)(c), ICJ Statute (1945) in order to reach decisions that concern international law. (See Chapter 2.)

National law principles may be very closely related to international legal rights/obligations. For example, the concept of nationality originates in national law and the grant of nationality is a matter reserved for States. However, nationality may have implications for international law (e.g. diplomatic protection/State responsibility). The ICJ decided in the *Nottebohm Case (Liechtenstein v Guatemala)* (1955) that the grant of nationality must satisfy the requirements established by international law (the link between the national and the State seeking to exercise diplomatic protection must be both real and effective). (See Chapter 8.)

International courts may have to decide a case by reference to the national law of a State via an agreement between the State parties to that effect. See the *Brazilian Loans Case (France v Brazil)* (1929) and the *Serbian Loans Case (France v Serbia)* (1929).

However, national legal rules do not necessarily have the status of law within the international legal system (they are not deemed to be 'laws of the forum'). Instead they are accorded the status of 'facts' that can determine the application of international law. The PCIJ in the *Certain German Interests in Polish Upper Silesia Case* (1925) observed that: 'From the standpoint of International Law . . . municipal laws are merely facts which express the will and constitute the activities of States' (at 19). In particular, national legal rules may constitute evidence of compliance or non-compliance with international law.

However, when interpreting national law, international courts will have 'the utmost regard to the decisions of the municipal courts' (*Brazilian Loans Case*). International courts do not want to undermine the integrity of national laws. However, national laws cannot be legally binding as a matter of international law (as a State cannot make international law unilaterally).

■ Putting it all together

Answer guidelines

See the problem question at the start of the chapter.

Approaching the question

The question addresses the following key topics:

- theories about the relationship between international law and national law;
- concept of State sovereignty;
- doctrinal approaches to the reception of CIL rules into UK law;
- implications of a purported exercise of sovereign jurisdiction;
- state responsibility (Chapter 8).

▶

Important points to include

- You should discuss the consequences of the UK's dualist approach to the reception of international law into its domestic law in general.
- Is the rule an established CIL rule?
- If so, would the CIL rule be binding on the UK courts via the doctrine of incorporation (*R* v *Keyn*)?
- Does the UK have jurisdiction over the incident under the territorial principle of jurisdiction? *Mortensen* v *Peters* is authority for the proposition that the UK courts are bound to give effect to the clear provisions of a statute.
- If the UK is bound by the CIL rule, discuss implications of the conflict between an Act of Parliament and a CIL rule. Under the principle of parliamentary sovereignty the Act should prevail from the perspective of UK law.
- Does the UK have jurisdiction over the incident under the nationality principle? The ships are not registered in the UK and none of the persons involved is a UK national.

 Make your answer stand out

- Could it be argued that the UK is not bound by the CIL rule in question by virtue of the persistent objector (*Anglo-Norwegian Fisheries*)? If successful this argument would enable the UK to exercise jurisdiction over the captain according to the territorial principle.
- The Act would appear to constitute valid UK law but, as it conflicts with an established CIL rule, the UK would seem to be liable to a claim of international responsibility before the ICJ.
- This is a good example of the Fitzmaurice compromise.

READ TO IMPRESS

Capps, P. (2007) 'The Court as Gatekeeper: Customary International Law in English Courts', 70 *MLR* 558.

Denza, D. (2010) 'The Relationship between International Law and National Law', in M. Evans (ed.) *International Law*, 3rd edn. Oxford University Press.

Nijman, J. E. (2007) *New Perspectives on the Divide Between National and International Law*. Oxford University Press.

Sales, P. and Clement, J. (2008) 'International Law in Domestic Courts: The Developing Framework', *LQR* 388.

www.pearsoned.co.uk/lawexpress

Go online to access more revision support including quizzes to test your knowledge, sample questions with answer guidelines, podcasts you can download, and more!

Jurisdiction and immunity

6

Revision checklist

Essential points you should know:

- ☐ Connection between sovereignty and jurisdiction
- ☐ Difference between prescriptive and enforcement jurisdiction
- ☐ Principles of jurisdiction
- ☐ State immunity from criminal jurisdiction
- ☐ State immunity from civil jurisdiction

■ Topic map

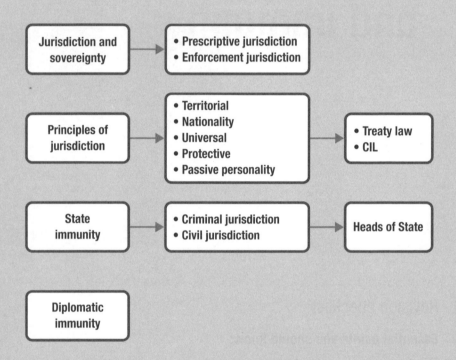

■ Introduction

Sovereignty can be defined as a bundle of rights, privileges and obligations possessed by States. The topic of jurisdiction provides an excellent illustration of sovereignty in action and it will be considered in the first part of this chapter. It will then consider situations where a State may be able to claim immunity from the exercise of jurisdiction by another State as a result of the notion of sovereign equality.

ASSESSMENT ADVICE

Essay questions

Essay questions often focus on the principles of jurisdiction. They may ask you to reflect on development of a particular principle or to challenge its application in a specific case. You will need to appreciate the strengths and weaknesses of each principle and develop a good knowledge of the key examples mentioned in this chapter.

Problem questions

These questions typically ask students to consider which of the principles of jurisdiction are applicable in a given scenario. The principles of jurisdiction overlap and so it is helpful if you can show how they might work together to support a particular jurisdictional claim. It is important to demonstrate a good knowledge of the relevant case law in this context.

■ Sample question

Could you answer this question? Below is a typical problem question that could arise on this topic. Guidelines on answering the question are included at the end of this chapter, whilst a sample essay question and guidance on tackling it can be found on the companion website.

PROBLEM QUESTION

Two nationals of State A decide to plant an explosive device on a commercial aircraft belonging to an airline registered in State B. The device is planted in State C, it explodes over State D, killing all those on board (the majority were nationals of State B). The offenders are currently residing in State Y. Their actions violate the Montréal Convention for the Suppression of Unlawful Acts against the Safety of Civil Aircraft (1971). States B, C and Y are parties to the 1971 Convention. Which States would have a claim to jurisdiction in order to prosecute the offenders under international law? Further, on what grounds would they have the right to claim jurisdiction?

■ Jurisdiction and sovereignty

A State's entitlement to exercise jurisdiction is a consequence of its sovereignty. However, a State's sovereignty is limited by the sovereignty of other States (through the notion of sovereign equality). Consequently, State sovereignty is essentially a territorial concept. A State is sovereign within its own territory and it can exercise jurisdiction exclusively within it (see Chapter 7). It follows from this that States must respect the sovereignty of other States (they do not have the right to exercise their jurisdiction within the territory of another State). This approach to sovereignty and jurisdiction recognises that the international legal system is made up of independent sovereign States and organised on a horizontal basis (see Chapter 1).

> **KEY INSTRUMENT**
>
> **Article 2(7), UN Charter**
>
> 'Nothing contained in the present Charter shall authorize the United Nations to intervene in matters which are essentially within the domestic jurisdiction of any State or shall require the Members to submit such matters to settlement under the present Charter . . .'

However, jurisdiction cannot be limited to a territorial concept because a State's interests extend beyond its borders.

> **! Don't be tempted to . . .**
>
> Don't confuse the concept of State jurisdiction with the notion of a court's jurisdiction to adjudicate cases. (The latter will be considered in Chapter 9.)

It is readily assumed that States are entitled to exercise jurisdiction within their own territory. However, beyond that, it is clear that States have to *claim* jurisdiction. Not all States claim jurisdiction to the same extent. Whether a State decides to claim jurisdiction in a given situation will depend on its national interests and its resources. States typically make jurisdictional claims in their national legislation but they may also claim jurisdiction by reference to the established principles of international law (see below).

Jurisdiction can be divided into **prescriptive jurisdiction** and **enforcement jurisdiction**.

Prescriptive jurisdiction

> **KEY DEFINITION: Prescriptive jurisdiction**
>
> Prescriptive jurisdiction is concerned with a State's capacity to legislate for certain persons and in certain situations.

KEY CASE

The Lotus Case (1927) PCIJ Series A, No. 10

Concerning: criminal jurisdiction regarding a collision on the High Seas
Legal issue: the nature and extent of prescriptive jurisdiction

Facts

A French ship collided with a Turkish ship on the High Seas. The collision caused the Turkish ship to sink, and resulted in the loss of life. The French ship sailed to a Turkish port where a French Officer was charged with manslaughter by the Turkish authorities.

Legal principle

The PCIJ made the following observation on the nature and extent of prescriptive jurisdiction:

> 'Far from laying down a general prohibition to the effect that States may not extend the application of their laws and the jurisdiction of their courts to persons, property and acts outside their territory, [international law] leaves them in this respect a wide measure of discretion' (at 19).

A State's interests extend beyond its boundaries. Consequently, international law recognises that States possess extensive *prescriptive* jurisdiction. A State could enact legislation that seeks to bind persons outside its territory. However, there must be jurisdictional limits placed upon the exercise of a State's sovereign claims otherwise there is a danger that they would interfere with the sovereignty of other States. Consequently, prescriptive jurisdiction is counterbalanced by the concept of *enforcement* jurisdiction.

Enforcement jurisdiction

KEY DEFINITION: Enforcement jurisdiction

Enforcement jurisdiction concerns a State's capacity to enforce its national laws in its own territory.

KEY CASE

The Lotus Case (1927) PCIJ Series A, No. 10

Concerning: criminal jurisdiction regarding a collision on the High Seas
Legal issue: the nature and extent of enforcement jurisdiction

Facts

See above.

▶

Legal principle

The PCIJ made the following observation on the nature and extent of enforcement jurisdiction:

'Now the first and foremost restriction imposed by international law upon a State is that . . . it may not exercise its power in any form in the territory of another State. In this sense jurisdiction is certainly territorial; it cannot be exercised by a State outside its territory . . .' (18–19).

Enforcement jurisdiction recognises that a State's authority is ultimately territorial. International law tries to achieve a balance between a State's ability to pursue its national interests and the national interests of other States. If international law did not draw a distinction between prescriptive and enforcement jurisdiction then States could claim jurisdiction in ways that would challenge the sovereignty of other States and thus undermine the basic principle of the international legal system.

📖 **REVISION NOTE**

Jurisdiction can be divided into criminal jurisdiction and civil jurisdiction. Criminal jurisdiction has been far more problematic and international law has paid far more attention to it as a result. Assessment questions typically focus solely upon criminal jurisdiction.

■ Principles of jurisdiction

Commentators have identified five principles concerning the exercise of criminal jurisdiction:

1 Territorial

2 Nationality

3 Universal

4 Protective

5 Passive personality.

These principles were developed by a group of American international lawyers. The Harvard Research Draft Convention on Criminal Jurisdiction (1935) adopted and endorsed the first four principles set out above. It reflected CIL in many respects. (See Chapter 2.)

1 Territorial jurisdiction

The territorial principle is the most fundamental principle for the exercise of jurisdiction. It is consistent with our common-sense understanding of the limits of a State's sovereign authority. For example, there is a presumption that UK statutes are not applicable outside UK territory.

But while the notion of territorial jurisdiction is usually limited to the national territory belonging to a State, in exceptional cases a State may exercise this form of jurisdiction in the territory of another State. This is commonly known as extraterritorial jurisdiction.

There have been a number of cases concerning extraterritorial jurisdiction under the European Convention on Human Rights (ECHR) (1950). Article 1 provides that: 'The High Contracting Parties shall secure to everyone within their jurisdiction the rights and freedoms defined in Section I of this Convention.' Originally, it was thought that the notion of State jurisdiction for the purpose of the application of the ECHR was limited to the combined European territory of the Contracting States. However, in a series of cases the European Court of Human Rights (ECtHR) has made it clear that the Convention can give rise to extraterritorial jurisdiction for Contracting States, in exceptional situations.

KEY CASE

Al-Skeini v *UK* (2011) 53 EHRR 18 ECtHR, App. No. 55721/07

Concerning: whether the UK's jurisdiction was engaged for the acts and/or omissions of British military forces during their occupation of Iraq in 2003

Facts

A number of Iraqi civilians were killed in the area: either they were shot in the streets or they died as a result of torture and one Iraqi was killed in a British military prison.

Legal principle

The Court decided that if a Contracting State exercised 'some of the public powers normally to be exercised by a sovereign government' in a place beyond its national territory, its jurisdiction may be engaged for alleged violations of the Convention where:

(a) it has 'effective control of the relevant territory and its inhabitants'; or

(b) its agents exercise 'authority and control' over the affected individuals.

It held that the deceased had come within the UK's jurisdiction under the authority and control of British military forces.

In most instances, a crime will be initiated and completed within the same jurisdiction. However, international law appreciates that a crime may have been initiated in one State but completed in another. This has led to the development of **objective** and **subjective** interpretations of the **territorial principle**.

KEY DEFINITION: Objective territorial principle

The objective territorial principle holds that a State has jurisdiction over a criminal offence that has been completed within its territory.

For example, in the *Lotus Case* a French ship crashed into a Turkish ship and so the alleged crime was completed on Turkish 'territory'.

KEY DEFINITION: Subjective territorial principle

The subjective territorial principle holds that a State has criminal jurisdiction in relation to an offence that was commenced in its territory but completed in the territory of another State.

KEY CASE

The Lockerbie Prosecutions (2001) 40 ILM 581

Concerning: the prosecution of the Lockerbie bombers
Legal issue: the exercise of the objective territorial principle of jurisdiction

Facts

In 1988, two Libyan nationals planted a bomb on a US-registered commercial aeroplane. It was planted in Malta. It exploded over Lockerbie in the UK killing 270 people. Article 1 Montréal Convention for the Suppression of Unlawful Acts against the Safety of Civil Aircraft (1971) makes it an offence to place a device on a civil aircraft which is likely to destroy or do damage to it. This provision was transformed into UK law by section 2 Aviation Security Act (1982).

Legal principle

The UK exercised jurisdiction via the objective territorial principle. The suspects were tried and convicted under Scottish law.

In the *Lockerbie Case*, the UK exercised jurisdiction under the objective territorial principle. However, Malta could have exercised jurisdiction under the subjective territorial principle because the offence was commenced there.

✎ EXAM TIP

An exception to the territorial principle (for the purpose of enforcement) may occur where States agree between themselves to permit one State to enforce its jurisdiction in the territory of another State. For instance, the *Lockerbie Case* was heard by a Scottish court sitting in the Netherlands pursuant to a 1998 UK–Dutch treaty. See Aust (2000). This exception illustrates the consent model of international law explored in Chapter 1.

---

2 Nationality jurisdiction

A State may choose to exercise jurisdiction over its nationals, wherever they may be. This power is a consequence of a State's duty to extend **diplomatic protection** to its nationals when they are within the territory of another State (see Chapter 8). However, while States have the power to exercise jurisdiction over their nationals, they usually only do so when a criminal offence has the capacity to affect their national interests. For example, Earl Russell was convicted of bigamy in the UK courts for an offence that was committed in the US (*R* v *Earl Russell* [1901] AC 446).

3 Universal jurisdiction

Universal jurisdiction is based on the idea that some crimes are so serious that all States have an interest in their prosecution. Consequently, all States have jurisdiction regarding such crimes. In this sense, jurisdiction arises from 'community interest' rather than the 'national interest'.

The classical example of a crime which gives rise to universal jurisdiction is the crime of piracy. All States have a vested interest in preventing piracy. Moreover, as piracy typically occurs on the high seas, no State can have territorial jurisdiction over acts of piracy. Accordingly, international law recognises that all States have jurisdiction in relation to crimes of piracy because of the absence of territorial jurisdiction rather than because of the nature of this crime.

Most crimes occur within the territory of a single State and the primary principle of jurisdiction is the territorial principle. But what if a State does not wish to prosecute an offender present in its territory? What if the wrongdoer escapes to another State? Are some crimes so serious *in substance* that States, which are not directly affected by the criminal conduct in question, could have jurisdiction to prosecute the offender?

The issue of universal jurisdiction can be divided into treaty law and CIL.

Treaty law

States have recognised that they have a common interest in ensuring that serious crimes are prosecuted and that offenders cannot evade justice merely by crossing State boundaries. Consequently, multilateral treaties have been agreed which concern the jurisdiction to prosecute with regard to certain serious crimes. Many States have ratified treaties and some have near universal application. Examples include:

- UN Convention on the Prohibition against Torture (1984), which underpinned *R* v *Bow Street Metropolitan Stipendiary Magistrates, ex parte Pinochet Ugarte (No. 3)* [2000] 1 AC 147 (below);

- Montréal Convention for the Suppression of Unlawful Acts against the Safety of Civil Aircraft (1971), which underpinned the *Lockerbie Case* (2001).

These treaty-based crimes function on the basis of the legal obligation to prosecute or extradite the offender (*aut dedere aut judicare*). Treaties typically require State parties to make the international crime in question a criminal offence within their own national legal system; they obligate States to search their territory for persons suspected of these crimes and once apprehended to prosecute them according to their national law. Alternatively, States are under an obligation to extradite those persons to an interested State for the purpose of prosecution.

The growing network of multilateral treaties of this nature has meant that we can speak of a least quasi-universal treaty-based jurisdiction (or *subsidiary* universal jurisdiction). However, you must remember that jurisdiction in such cases is based on treaty law and that treaties are only binding on those States that are parties to them. (See Chapter 3.)

If an offender resides in a State that has not ratified the relevant treaty regime then other States will not have the jurisdiction to prosecute the offender if their own claim to jurisdiction is based on universality.

CIL

In the absence of an applicable multilateral treaty regime, is there universal jurisdiction to prosecute crimes in CIL?

KEY CASE

Attorney General of Israel v *Eichmann* (1961) 36 ILR 5

Concerning: the trial of Adolf Eichmann
Legal issue: how jurisdiction can be established by the universal principle

Facts

Eichmann was in charge of implementing the Nazi's policy of systematically exterminating the Jews during the Second World War. He was found in Argentina in 1960 and taken to Israel where he was prosecuted under the 1951 Israeli Law for war crimes and crimes against the Jewish people.

Legal principle

The Israeli court decided that Israel had the right to prosecute Eichmann because these offences were crimes of such a magnitude that they gave rise to universal jurisdiction as a matter of CIL.

In *Eichmann*, the court stated that:

> International law is, in the absence of an International Court, in need of the judicial and legislative organs of every country to give effect to its criminal interdictions and to bring the criminals to trial (Para. 12).

 Make your answer stand out

Does the creation of the ICC undermine the scope for States to claim that they have universal criminal jurisdiction? Does it supplement their capacity to invoke universal jurisdiction or does it supersede States' jurisdictional claims? You should reflect on the nature of the ICC and the scope of its powers and whether it intended to diminish States' sovereign powers. See the ICJ's decision in *Arrest Warrant Case* (2002) (below).

KEY CASE

Arrest Warrant Case (2002) ICJ Rep 3

Concerning: use of universal jurisdiction to arrest a Foreign Minister
Legal issue: the limits of universal jurisdiction

Facts

A warrant was issued for the arrest of the Congo's Foreign Minister (*in absentia*). It alleged that he had committed war crimes and crimes against humanity. A 1993 Belgian law gave the Belgian authorities jurisdiction to prosecute such crimes wherever they may have been committed. In response, Congo instituted proceedings against Belgium.

Legal principle

The ICJ decided that Congo's Foreign Minister was entitled to be protected by the doctrine of State immunity. Consequently, Belgium had no jurisdiction to arrest and to prosecute him.

In a Joint Separate Opinion delivered in the *Arrest Warrant Case*, three judges considered Belgium's claim of universal jurisdiction. The Joint Opinion noted that international law was silent on whether universal jurisdiction could be exercised *in absentia*. However, it suggested that, in principle, international law does not prohibit the exercise of universal jurisdiction in such a case. The Joint Opinion justified its view by reference to the *Lotus* principle – freedom of action unless it can be shown that such freedom has been restricted by international law (leaving aside the question of State immunity – see below).

 Make your answer stand out

To what extent is it still helpful to invoke the *Lotus* principle to justify the actions of States where international law has sought to regulate the area in question? ICJ President Guillaume questioned whether reliance on the *Lotus* principle in support of universal jurisdiction is justified given the developments in international criminal law. Read the Opinions delivered in the *Arrest Warrant Case*.

4 Protective jurisdiction

The protective principle holds that States have the right to exercise jurisdiction for crimes committed abroad if the criminal activity in question harms their vital interests.

Figure 6.1

Claiming universal jurisdiction

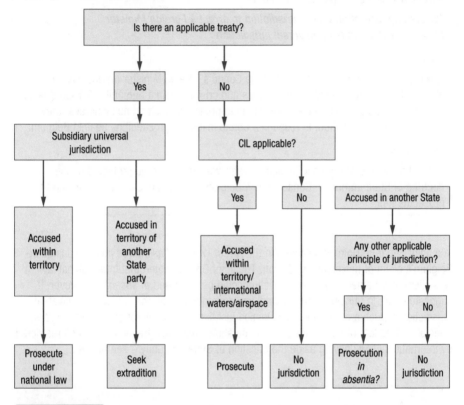

DPP v *Joyce* [1946] AC 347 (HL)

Concerning: prosecution for criminal offences committed abroad

Facts

Joyce made propaganda radio broadcasts from Germany on behalf of the German government during the Second World War. He was a US national who lived in the UK. He had obtained a UK passport fraudulently. He was arrested and tried for treason in the UK.

Legal principle

A State has the right to exercise jurisdiction to prosecute an alien for a crime that was committed abroad if the criminal activity threatens its security. However, there must be some connection between the accused and that State. The passport provided that link. The HL decided that, as the accused was entitled to protection from the UK, it was entitled to expect allegiance in return.

KEY CASE

Attorney of Israel v *Eichmann* (1961) 36 ILR 5

Concerning: the trial of Adolf Eichmann
Legal issue: how jurisdiction can be established by reference to the protective
principle of jurisdiction

Facts

In addition to claiming the jurisdiction to prosecute Eichmann via the universal principle of jurisdiction, Israel also justified its actions by reference to the protective jurisdiction principle.

Legal principle

The Israeli court decided that a State could invoke the protective principle when its interests were affected to a greater extent that those of other States. On the facts, it found that the activities of the accused exhibited a fundamental connection with the Jewish people and thus gave rise to a legitimate exercise of protective jurisdiction.

 Make your answer stand out

Israel did not exist as a State until 1948. Could Israel justify its exercise of jurisdiction via the protective principle in *Eichmann*? You should consider the connection between the interests of a State and its people and the justifications for retroactive penal legislation. Read Steiner, Alston and Goodman (2008) on the Nuremberg Trials (115–129).

5 Passive personality jurisdiction

The passive personality principle focuses on the nationality of the *victim*. The passive personality was not endorsed by the Harvard Draft Convention and its status as a principle of jurisdiction is still controversial today.

KEY CASE

Cutting's Case (1886) Moore, Digest of International Law, vol. ii, 228

Concerning: prosecution of a US national for a violation of Mexican law perpetrated in the US

Facts

Cutting was a US national and the editor of a US publication. He was arrested during a visit to Mexico and was prosecuted under a Mexican law that made it a criminal offence to libel a Mexican national wherever the libel occurred. The publication in question had not been circulated in Mexico. ▶

Legal principle

The US government protested that, on the facts, a claim of jurisdiction justified by the passive personality principle was wrong. In response to this protest Cutting was released by the Mexican authorities. This case shows that the passive personality principle has not been generally accepted as a legitimate ground for the exercise of State jurisdiction.

In the *Lotus Case* (1927), Judge Moore said that the passive personality principle:

> means that the citizen of one country, when he visits another country, takes with him for his 'protection' the law of his own country and subjects those with whom he comes into contact to the operation of that law.

For this reason, States have been very reluctant to endorse the principle. However, they have relied on it in exceptional cases.

KEY CASE

US v *Yunis (No. 2)* **(1991) 30 ILM 463**

Concerning: the prosecution of an aircraft hijacker in the US

Facts

In 1985, a Lebanese national hijacked a Jordanian plane at Beirut airport. The plane was subsequently blown up, killing the passengers on board. Two of the passengers were US nationals. US security agents arrested the defendant in international waters. He stood trial in a US court.

Legal principle

The court found that the US had jurisdiction under the passive personality principle. It decided that the principle could be invoked exceptionally in respect of 'serious and universally condemned crimes' that would not increase the risk of criminal liability in general.

✎ EXAM TIP

In *Eichmann*, Israel claimed jurisdiction under the universal and protective principles. In *Yunis*, the US claimed that it was entitled to exercise jurisdiction via the universal and passive personality principles. When States seek to make a claim of universal jurisdiction why do they also claim jurisdiction by reference to another principle of jurisdiction as well? Is it because universal jurisdiction provides a very weak basis for a claim of State jurisdiction? See the *Arrest Warrant Case* (2002).

Make your answer stand out

Are the five principles of jurisdiction hierarchical? Does jurisdiction depend on the whereabouts of the accused and the willingness of States to prosecute? See Lowe and Staker (2010).

■ State immunity

Immunity from criminal jurisdiction

It follows from the notion of sovereign equality that all States must recognise the sovereignty of other States. A State must not exercise jurisdiction in a way that would compromise the sovereignty of another State.

States can only act through their representatives. Consequently, if government officials are obstructed in the exercise of State functions then, in effect, the State itself is being obstructed. In such cases a State's sovereignty is being endangered by another State. This danger has led to the development of certain immunities from the exercise of jurisdiction.

Heads of State

The rules concerning **immunity (*ratione personae* and ratione materiae)** for Heads of State arise from CIL.

> **KEY DEFINITION: Immunity *ratione personae***
>
> Serving Heads of State enjoy absolute immunity from the exercise of criminal jurisdiction by the courts of another State.

This follows from the assumption that a serving Head of State is, in effect, the embodiment of his or her State. No State can exercise sovereignty over the Head of another State.

> **KEY DEFINITION: Immunity *ratione materiae***
>
> Former Heads of State are entitled to functional immunity from the exercise of criminal jurisdiction by the courts of another State in certain situations.

In certain situations, a former Head of State will enjoy ongoing immunity for his or her actions during the period he or she was in office. The justification for this form of immunity is based on protecting the State. If international law allowed States to prosecute former Heads of States for everything they did while they were in office then the sovereignty of the State they served would be indirectly compromised. Serving Heads of State would be mindful of the possibility of prosecution by another State if they travelled abroad after they left office and this will affect their ability to perform their State functions properly.

However, it should be noted that the scope of functional immunity only protects the former Head of State for the *legitimate* State functions they performed during their term of office.

KEY CASE

R v Bow Street Magistrates, ex parte Pinochet (No. 3) [2000] 1 AC 147

Concerning: immunity of a former Head of State from criminal jurisdiction of another State

Facts

Pinochet was a former Chilean Head of State. He visited the UK for medical treatment. While in the UK, Spain requested his extradition for acts of torture committed during his period of office. The UK, Spain and Chile had ratified the Torture Convention (1984). The Convention contained an *aut dedere aut judicare* provision. The UK courts had to decide whether Pinochet had immunity from prosecution as a matter of international law.

Legal principle

As Pinochet was a former Head of State he was not entitled to personal immunity from prosecution. The key question was whether he enjoyed functional immunity (*ratione materiae*) in relation to the alleged offences. The HL decided that torture could not be classified as a legitimate State function. Accordingly, Pinochet was not protected by functional immunity and he was liable to extradition.

✎ EXAM TIP

It is easy to see why torture is not classified as official State business. However, the distinction between official and private acts is not always easy to pinpoint. You should reflect on the limits of functional immunity and the extent of the protection that should be afforded to former Heads of State.

KEY CASE

Arrest Warrant Case (2002) ICJ Rep 3

Concerning: use of universal jurisdiction to arrest a Foreign Minister
Legal issue: the nature and scope of the doctrine of State immunity from criminal proceedings

Facts

See above.

Legal principle

The ICJ held that the Democratic Republic of Congo's Foreign Minister was entitled to immunity *ratione personae* (complete personal immunity) from the criminal jurisdiction of another State because he was a serving senior minister at the time the arrest warrant was issued.

 Make your answer stand out

In the *Arrest Warrant Case*, the ICJ extended the scope of State immunity to include foreign ministers. Arguably, foreign ministers should be immune from prosecution by the States given that the position is widely recognised as a major office of State. Moreover, they have to travel extensively in order to perform their functions on behalf of their respective States. Nonetheless, how far do you think the plea of State immunity should extend?

You should appreciate that pleas of State immunity do not prevent a State from exercising criminal jurisdiction over its own Head of State. For example, Chile could have decided to prosecute Pinochet in its national courts.

Immunity from civil jurisdiction

State immunity can also be claimed against the exercise of *civil* jurisdiction by another State. Traditionally, international law endorsed the concept of absolute immunity in this regard.

KEY CASE

The Parlement Belge (1879–80) LR 5 PD 197

Concerning: a claim of absolute immunity in response to a civil claim
Legal issue: the extent of a claim of State immunity in response to a civil claim

Facts

The *Parlement Belge* was a ship owned by the Belgian king. It collided with an English boat which sustained damage as a result. The owner sued the Belgian king in the UK courts. A claim of absolute sovereign immunity was made. If the immunity claim were successful then the court would have no jurisdiction to decide the case.

Legal principle

The Court of Appeal decided that the appropriate test was that of absolute immunity.

KEY CASE

Germany v *Italy* **(Jurisdictional Immunities of States) (2012) ICJ**

Concerning: whether States enjoy immunity from the jurisdiction of the national courts of other States

Facts

Italian courts decided that civil proceedings could be instituted against Germany for the criminal behaviour of its military forces during the Second World War. Further, they also held that certain civil judgments decided by the Greek national courts could be enforced by the Italian courts. The ICJ had to decide whether Germany enjoyed immunity in such situations.

Legal principle

The ICJ held that States enjoy immunity from the jurisdiction of the national courts of other States even in situations where peremptory norms of international law have been violated. Further, it decided that States enjoy immunity from the enforcement of judgments entered by the national courts of other States. Accordingly, on both issues, the ICJ decided that the Italian national courts had contravened international law and Germany could rely on the doctrine of State immunity.

International law has moved away from recognising that States have absolute immunity towards the concept of relative State immunity. Relative immunity draws a distinction between public acts done by States in exercise of their sovereign authority (*jure imperii*) and private or commercial acts that are undertaken by States (*jure gestionis*).

✎ EXAM TIP

You should appreciate that the doctrine of relative immunity is not without its problems. Courts are now willing to acknowledge that a State (acting through its courts) may exercise jurisdiction over another State in relation to civil proceedings. However, a forum or host State has no jurisdiction to enforce the judgment of a court against another State.

KEY CASE

Trendtex Trading v *Central Bank of Nigeria* **[1977] QB 529**

Concerning: a claim of State immunity for the debts of the government body
Legal issue: how jurisdiction can arise when a claim of State immunity is made in a civil case

Facts

Trendtex sold cement to the Nigerian government to be used in the construction of public buildings. The government instructed its central bank not to pay for the cement.

Trendtex sued the bank in the UK courts. The bank made a claim of absolute State immunity. If the claim were successful, the UK court would not have jurisdiction over the dispute.

Legal principle

The court held that the CIL rule concerning absolute immunity had been replaced by a new CIL rule of restrictive State immunity where the State was engaged in commercial activity.

Absolute State immunity made sense in a time when States only acted in a public capacity. However, during the twentieth century, States began to engage more and more in commercial projects. When States acted in such a private capacity they were acting as ordinary legal persons. However, allowing States to have absolute immunity in such situations was unfair to the other (non-State) party as they could not institute legal proceedings against a State. Accordingly, international law began to endorse the relative approach to State immunity in civil cases.

Figure 6.2
Sovereign authority and sovereign equality

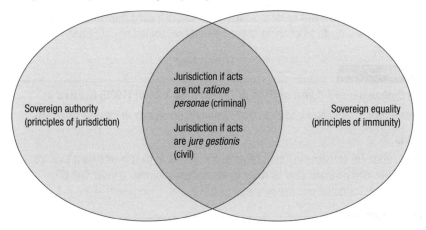

Sovereign authority
(principles of jurisdiction)

Jurisdiction if acts are not *ratione personae* (criminal)

Jurisdiction if acts are *jure gestionis* (civil)

Sovereign equality
(principles of immunity)

■ Diplomatic immunity

Diplomats carry out public functions on behalf of their States. Consequently, diplomatic immunity is an important practical aspect of State immunity. The topic of diplomatic immunity, like the forms of State immunity discussed above, is based on the interrelationship between sovereign authority and sovereign equality. It is largely governed by the Vienna Convention on Diplomatic Relations (1961).

KEY INSTRUMENT

Article 29 Vienna Convention on Diplomatic Relations (1961)

'The person of the diplomatic agent shall be inviolable. He shall not be liable for any form of arrest or detention. The receiving State shall treat him with due respect and shall take all appropriate steps to prevent any attack on his person, freedom, or dignity.'

Diplomatic agents enjoy personal immunity from criminal prosecution in the courts of the receiving State. In addition, diplomatic agents also enjoy immunity from civil proceedings save for situations where an agent is acting beyond his or her official functions or in a purely private capacity (Art. 21).

It should be noted that the personal immunity of diplomatic agents is part of the wider set of diplomatic privileges and immunities enjoyed by States in the territory of the receiving State. These include immunity of diplomatic premises (Art. 22), archives and documents (Art. 24), and official correspondence, including the 'diplomatic bag' (Art. 27).

States very rarely infringe the rules relating to diplomatic immunity because all States will invariably be both receiving and sending States for the purpose of diplomatic immunity. Accordingly, if a State decided to violate the diplomatic privileges and immunities of other States in its own territory, it would render its own diplomatic premises and staff vulnerable to corresponding treatment in other States. This area is a good illustration of reciprocity that is central to the smooth functioning of the international community of States.

KEY CASE

US Diplomatic and Consular Staff in Tehran (*USA* v *Iran*) (1980) ICJ Rep 3
Concerning: The nature and extent of diplomatic immunity in international law

Facts

In 1979 the US embassy in Tehran was overrun by local people who then took US diplomatic and consular staff hostage in the embassy for over a year. The US government instituted proceedings against the Iranian government at the ICJ.

Legal principle

The ICJ decided that the Iranian government had failed to protect the US diplomatic and consular premises and staff in violation of Article 29 of the Vienna Convention on Diplomatic Relations (1961).

The recognition of immunity of diplomatic agents does not mean that the host State has to tolerate the actions of diplomatic agents where such behaviour contravenes its national law. It can always dismiss an agent from its national territory (Art. 9). Further, in grave cases, it has the option of breaking off the diplomatic relations with the sending State.

KEY CASE

Julian Assange (2012) v *Swedish Prosecution Authority* [2012] UKSC 22
Concerning: the limits of claims of diplomatic immunity

Facts

Assange, the founder of Wiki-leaks, was the subject of a European arrest warrant concerning sexual offence charges in Sweden. The UK Supreme Court decided that he must be extradited to Sweden pursuant to these charges. However, Assange claimed that, once in Sweden, he would be at risk of being extradited to the US, where he feared that he would be prosecuted for his political activities. On 19 June 2012, Assange breached his bail conditions and sought diplomatic asylum in Ecuador's embassy in London. The Ecuadorian government granted him asylum. The UK government demanded that Assange be handed over into its custody. Ecuador refused to comply with this demand and a diplomatic stand-off ensued.

Legal principle

Article 22 of the 1961 Convention provides that embassies are inviolable and so British agents could not enter Ecuador's embassy without the agreement of the government of Ecuador.

But was Assange entitled to claim diplomatic asylum as a matter of international law? The Refugee Convention (1951) recognises that a *State* is entitled to grant asylum in certain circumstances. Under Article 1 of the 1951 Convention, a person cannot rely on the Convention if he or she has committed a serious non-political crime before claiming asylum. Assange has been charged with serious non-political offences and so it appears that his claim for asylum is compromised as a matter of international law.

Further, if a State decides to grant asylum it would typically allow the claimant to enter its territory *directly*. However, Assange did not seek *direct* entry to Ecuador's territory. He sought to gain asylum by entering Ecuador's embassy in the UK, which is situated on British soil. As a result, the UK government is *not* required to grant Assange safe passage so that he can leave British territory. It would appear that Assange's claim for asylum would fail as a matter of international law.

 Make your answer stand out

This case is important because, in effect, Ecuador used the diplomatic immunity conferred on its embassy by international law in order to interfere in the operation of the British criminal justice system. Consequently, Assange's case provides a good example of the tension that exists between, on the one hand, the exercise of one sovereign State's jurisdiction in its own territory and, on the other hand, the principles of immunity that have been developed in international law to protect the sovereign equality of all States.

✎ **EXAM TIP**

If you were confronted with an exam question based on the Assange case, you would need to demonstrate a good understanding of the legal issues which have just been raised. However, in order to do well you would also need to explore the broader implications of this notorious case for international law. Even though Assange's claim of diplomatic asylum is not recognised as a matter of international law, Ecuador did grant him asylum. What does Assange's case tell us about the relationship between law and international politics? (See Chapter 1 for guidance on this fundamental issue.)

■ Putting it all together

Answer guidelines

See the problem question at the start of the chapter.

Approaching the question

To answer this question you will need to address the following key topics:

- relationship between jurisdiction and sovereignty;
- principles of jurisdiction;
- treaty-based subsidiary universal jurisdiction.

Important points to include

- Introduce the nature of jurisdictional claims to show how they are manifestations of sovereignty.
- Identify and explain the difference between prescriptive and enforcement jurisdiction.
- Explain the principles of jurisdiction and apply them to the question:
  - □ State C can rely upon the subjective territorial principle because the crime was started in its territory.
  - □ State D can rely upon the objective territorial principle because the crime was completed in its territory (*Lockerbie*).
  - □ State A could invoke the nationality principle because the offenders are its nationals (*Russell*).

- □ State B could invoke the passive personality principle because its nationals are the victims of the crime (*Yunis*).

- □ Could State B also rely upon the protective principle? You would need to establish a connection between the offenders and State B (*Eichmann* and *Joyce*).

 Make your answer stand out

- To what extent could all the States concerned with this crime invoke universal jurisdiction?

- Under treaty law, States B, C and Y are parties to the 1971 Convention, which provides for prosecution or extradition for Convention crimes. State Y should prosecute or allow for the extradition of the offenders to either State B or State C (if they make a request for extradition).

- Could any other State invoke universal jurisdiction to prosecute the crime? You would need to consider whether it was a crime under CIL and whether the case law supports such a jurisdictional claim. You would need to analyse *Eichmann* and the *Arrest Warrant Case*.

READ TO IMPRESS

Akehurst, M. (1972–73) 'Jurisdiction in International Law', 46 *BYIL* 146.

Aust, A. (2000) 'Lockerbie: The Other Case', *ICLQ* 278.

Besson, S. 'The Extraterritoriality of the ECHR' (2012) 25 *Leiden JIL* 857.

Den Heijer, M. 'Diplomatic Asylum and the Assange Case' (2013) 26 *Leiden JIL* 399.

Harvard Research Draft Convention on Criminal Jurisdiction (1935) 29 *AJIL Supp.* 443.

Lowe, V. and Staker, C. (2010) 'Jurisdiction,' in M. Evans (ed.) *International Law*, 3rd edn. Oxford University Press.

Steiner, H. I., Alston, P. and Goodman, R. (eds) (2008) *International Human Rights in Context*, 3rd edn. Oxford University Press.

www.pearsoned.co.uk/lawexpress

 Go online to access more revision support including quizzes to test your knowledge, sample questions with answer guidelines, podcasts you can download, and more!

Territory and self-determination

7

Revision checklist

Essential points you should know:

- [ ] Concept of territorial sovereignty
- [ ] Modes of territorial acquisition
- [ ] Nature of the right to self-determination
- [ ] Relationship between territory and self-determination
- [ ] Restrictions on claims of territorial sovereignty

Topic map

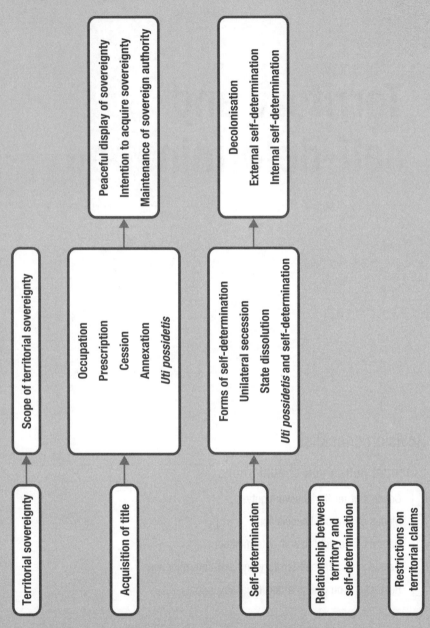

A printable version of this topic map is available from **www.pearsoned.co.uk/lawexpress**

■ Introduction

Territory gives the concept of sovereignty physical expression. Together, they provide the building blocks of the international legal system. However, the nature of their relationship has changed as a result of the rise of the right to self-determination. This chapter considers how the relationship between sovereignty, territory and self-determination has evolved in recent times.

ASSESSMENT ADVICE

Questions on territory and self-determination often concentrate on the difficult relationship between the exercise of the right to self-determination and the stability provided by established territorial units. It is important to develop a good understanding of these areas and of how they influence one another. There have been a number of significant judicial decisions in these areas and you should familiarise yourself with them. The topics covered in this chapter are contextual in nature. Do not simply discuss the relevant general principles without regard for the circumstances of a particular situation.

■ Sample question

Could you answer this question? Below is a typical problem question that could arise on this topic. Guidelines on answering the question are included at the end of this chapter, whilst a sample essay question and guidance on tackling it can be found on the companion website.

PROBLEM QUESTION

Arcadia, a group of islands, was discovered and colonised by Omega in the seventeenth century. In 1825, Omega transferred Acardia to Ruritania by treaty. Beta, one of the Arcadian islands, was unknown to either Omega or Ruritania at this time. It had been discovered and settled by Xenon in 1750. Ruritania found Beta in 1933. It immediately claimed sovereignty over the island via the 1825 treaty. Xenon has rejected Ruritania's claim. In 2011, Xenon held an election in Beta. Beta's inhabitants were given the choice of establishing their own State or remaining part of Xenon. The Betans decided to remain part of Xenon. Advise Ruritania whether Xenon has acquired valid title to Beta and about the implications of the 2011 election for its own claim to the island.

■ Territorial sovereignty

KEY DEFINITION: Territorial sovereignty

'Sovereignty in the relations between States signifies independence. Independence in regard to a portion of the globe is the right to exercise therein, to the exclusion of any other State, the functions of the State.' Huber J in the *Island of Palmas Case* (1928) 22 AJIL 867, 838.

□ REVISION NOTE

It is important to understand that sovereignty is not in absolute concept. The rules of international law constrain the exercise of State sovereignty in numerous ways. For example, international human rights law has created international legal obligations that affect the way that States can behave (even within their domestic jurisdictions). (See Chapter 1.)

Scope of territorial sovereignty

A State's 'territory' extends beyond the land mass itself to encompass the 'territorial sea' (which extends to a point 12 miles from the low-water mark) and the super adjacent airspace.

The concept of **territorial sovereignty** also applies to ships and aircraft that are registered to a State. For example, in the *Lotus Case* (1927), even though the collision occurred on the High Seas, the PCIJ held that, for the purposes of international law, it occurred on Turkish territory because the French ship crashed into the Turkish ship.

■ Acquisition of territory

If a State can show that it is exercising the functions of a State in a territory to the exclusion of other States then it can claim to have acquired sovereign authority over that territory.

International law has recognised a number of 'modes' of territorial acquisition. The most significant are:

- ■ Occupation
- ■ Prescription
- ■ Cession
- ■ Annexation

Occupation

KEY DEFINITION: Occupation

Occupation arises where a piece of territory is settled and claimed on behalf of a State.

Occupation is known as an *original* mode of acquisition because the territory in question has not previously been claimed and settled by another State. A State can claim the territory because it has not previously been subject to a sovereign claim – it is territory that belongs to no one (*terra nullius*). Consequently, the territory is capable of being acquired as long as a claimant State occupies it effectively.

 Make your answer stand out

International law is often defined as the law that governs relations between States. Until the colonial era, large parts of the world remained unclaimed by States. However, many areas were inhabited by organised social groups that were not recognised as States. Did these social groups possess sovereignty over the territories that they inhabited? Classical international law treated such groups as though they were incapable of acquiring territorial sovereignty and therefore their territories were open to acquisition by States via occupation. For an analysis of the concept of *terra nullius* in the colonial context see the *Western Sahara Case* (1975) ICJ Rep 12 and *Mabo v Queensland (No. 2)* (1992).

KEY CASE

Island of Palmas Case (1928) 22 AJIL 867

Concerning: a sovereignty dispute over territory
Legal issue: how title to territory can be acquired in international law by occupation

Facts

Spain transferred the Philippines to the US by the Treaty of Paris 1898. In 1906, the US found the Island of Palmas. It claimed that it had acquired sovereignty over the Island by the 1898 Treaty. However, the Netherlands argued that it had already acquired sovereignty over the Island.

Legal principle

The Arbitrator decided that the Netherlands had acquired the territory by means of occupation. It had established 'the continuous and peaceful display of territorial sovereignty' over the Island. In particular, the Netherlands could demonstrate an unchallenged connection to the territory evidenced by a series of administrative acts that had been carried out from the eighteenth century onwards.

Peaceful display of sovereignty

To acquire territory by way of occupation a State must be able to show that it controls the territory effectively. It must be able to demonstrate that it is exercising the functions of a State in that territory, but what are the functions of a State? They depend on the nature of the territory in question (e.g. a claim to a remote, uninhabited island may be supported by the carrying out of very few administrative acts). What really matters is whether a claimant State is publicly and peacefully behaving like a sovereign authority (e.g. by setting up of administrative systems).

KEY CASE

***Eastern Greenland Case* (1933) PCIJ Rep Series A/B No. 53, 46**
Concerning: a sovereignty dispute over Eastern Greenland

Facts

Denmark claimed territorial sovereignty over Greenland. However, in 1931, this claim was challenged by Norway in respect of Eastern Greenland.

Legal principle

The PCIJ upheld Denmark's claim. It observed that, in relation to sparsely populated or uninhabited territories, 'in many cases the tribunal has been satisfied with very little in the way of actual exercise of sovereign rights, provided that the other State could not make out a superior claim' (at 46). Denmark's claim was supported by evidence that it had granted trading concessions in Eastern Greenland and it had extended its national laws to the territory.

 Make your answer stand out

In the *Eastern Greenland Case*, the Court noted the relative nature of territorial disputes. It suggested that the party with the strongest claim to sovereignty will prevail. However, should international courts be willing to apportion territory based on very limited evidence? What if a State that was not a party to the case had a better claim? You should consider whether a court-based approach is the best way of resolving territorial disputes which may have consequences for the international community as a whole and whether the binding nature of judicial decisions means that States are reluctant to submit their territorial disputes to international courts.

> **!** **Don't be tempted to . . .**
>
> The peaceful display of sovereignty means that occupation is acquired peacefully in relation to other States (i.e. without being interrupted or disturbed by another State). It does not mean that States must remain peaceful in general or in their relations with their own nationals (although States may be subject to certain international legal obligations in this regard).

Intention to acquire sovereignty

Usually, if a State acts as though it has sovereign authority over a particular territory it will be readily presumed that it manifests an intention to behave in such a manner. Consequently, it is usually unnecessary to establish an intention to acquire territorial sovereignty. However, such intention becomes more important in situations where it is difficult to establish adequate physical displays of territorial sovereignty.

KEY CASE

Clipperton Island Arbitration **(1932) 26 AJIL 390**

Concerning: a sovereignty dispute over Clipperton Island

Facts

Clipperton Island was remote and uninhabited. In 1858, a French representative landed on the Island and claimed sovereignty over it on behalf of France. Subsequently, the French government published its claim in a regional journal. No manifestations of French sovereign authority were left on Clipperton Island. However, France maintained its claim over the years. Mexico subsequently claimed that the island had been discovered by Spain and that title had passed to it.

Legal principle

The Arbitrator decided that the island was unclaimed territory (*terra nullius*) before the French arrived in 1858. There was no evidence that it had been acquired by Spain. Although France had undertaken very few administrative acts in relation to Clipperton Island the publication of its claim was clear evidence of its intention to acquire sovereignty.

The continuous display of sovereignty

KEY CASE

Island of Palmas Case **(1928) 22 AJIL 867**
Concerning: a sovereignty dispute over territory
Legal issue: the relative nature of the exercise of sovereign authority over territory

Facts

See above.

Legal principle

'Manifestations of territorial sovereignty assume, it is true, different forms, according to conditions, time and place . . . The intermittence and discontinuity compatible with the maintenance of the right necessarily differ according as inhabited and or uninhabited regions are involved' (Huber J).

To establish valid title to territory, a State must be able to demonstrate that it has acquired the territory in conformity with international law and that its claim of territorial sovereignty has been maintained over time. In the context of occupation, a State must be able to show that it continues to control the territory in question effectively. Consequently, it must be able to demonstrate that its sovereign authority is being exercised in such a way that it is apparent to other States.

Prescription

KEY DEFINITION: Prescription

Prescription occurs where a State acquires title to territory by successfully displacing the sovereign authority of a State that has previously claimed sovereignty over that territory.

Prescription as a means of acquiring title to territory is similar to the mode of occupation. Both depend on a claimant State being able to demonstrate that it effectively controls the territory in issue. However, the key distinction between occupation and prescription is that, in the former, the territory had not previously been subject to a sovereign claim whereas, in the latter, a claimant State must be able to show that its claim has superseded the claim of the pre-existing territorial sovereign. Accordingly, a claimant State must be able to demonstrate:

1 'the continuous and peaceful display of territorial sovereignty' (*Island of Palmas Case*);

2   that it has exercised undisturbed sovereign authority over the territory in an open manner for a considerable period of time (*Kasikili/Sedudu Island Case* (1999) ICJ Rep 1045); and

3   that the pre-existing sovereign authority has acquiesced in the territorial claim of the claimant State – *Chamizal Arbitration* (1911) 5 AJIL 785.

The first requirement establishes that a claimant State is acting as though it were a sovereign authority. The second requirement enables the pre-existing sovereign authority to have the opportunity to challenge the development of a prescriptive claim. The final requirement establishes that the pre-existing sovereign authority has effectively abandoned its claim to the territory in question.

✎ EXAM TIP

It is important to understand the elements of both occupation and prescription and that you are able to show the differences between these two modes of acquisition. Given that occupation and prescription are grounded in the effective control of territory it is not surprising that they are typically pleaded together in litigation. For example, in the *Sovereignty over Pulau Litgitan and Pulau Sipadan (Indonesia* v *Malaysia)* (2002) ICJ Rep 625, Malaysia claimed that its predecessors had acquired valid title by occupation. However, it also claimed that it had displaced former sovereign authority by means of prescription.

Prescriptive claims have not been successfully advanced in international litigation, as yet. As long as the existing sovereign authority protests against the adverse claims and activities of a State seeking to advance a prescriptive claim, the courts will refuse to award the claimant State title to territory. See Figure 7.1.

Cession

KEY DEFINITION: Cession

Cession occurs where territory is transferred from one State to another State by treaty.

Cession is a *derivative* mode of territorial acquisition. It has been used extensively in international law. It has been commonly used in the following situations:

- to acquire colonial territory, e.g. the UK's acquisition of Hong Kong from China in 1842;

- as a means of expanding a State's territory, e.g. the US acquired Alaska from Russia in 1867; and

- as a component of peace treaties, e.g. Gibraltar was ceded to the UK as part of the Treaty of Utrecht 1713.

Figure 7.1

How occupation and prescription work

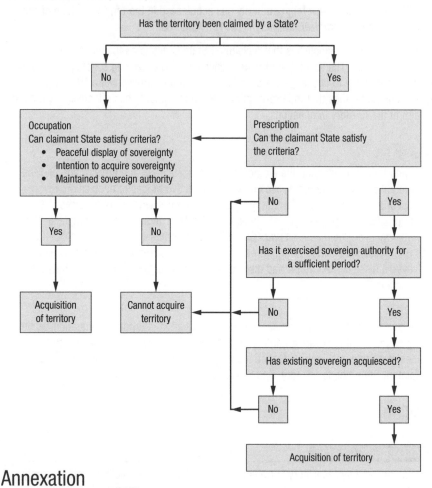

Annexation

KEY DEFINITION: Annexation

Annexation (or conquest) occurs where one State uses force to acquire territory belonging to another State.

This mode of acquisition is no longer recognised by international law. The Kellogg–Briand Pact (1928) condemned the resort to force as an instrument for the advancement of national policy or as a means of resolving international controversies. The prohibition on the use of force was strengthened by Article 2(4), UN Charter and it now has the status of a peremptory norm of international law. (See Chapter 10.)

KEY INSTRUMENT

Article 2(4) UN Charter

'All member States must refrain from the threat or use of force against the territorial integrity or political independence of any State.'

KEY INSTRUMENT

UN Declaration on Friendly Relations (1970)

'The territory of a State shall not be the object of acquisition by another State resulting from the threat or use of force. No territorial acquisition resulting from the threat or use of force shall be recognized as legal.'

📖 REVISION NOTE

A good example of the illegality of territorial annexation by the use of force is the invasion of Kuwait by Iraq in 1990 (see Chapter 10).

Uti possidetis juris

KEY DEFINITION: *Uti possidetis juris*

'New States will come to independence with the same boundaries they had when they were administrative units within the territory or territories of a colonial power.' Shaw (1996) 97.

To ensure international stability, international law endorsed the view that independence should, in principle, be achieved within existing (colonial) territorial units. Consequently, **uti possidetis juris** ensured that a post-colonial State would have the same territory as the colonial unit it replaced.

KEY CASE

The Frontier Dispute (1986) ICJ Rep 554

Concerning: a sovereignty dispute between Burkina Faso and Mali
Legal issue: the nature of the principle of uti possidetis *in international law*

Facts

The States of Burkina Faso and Mali achieved independence in 1960. They were previously French colonial territories. They shared a disputed frontier. They submitted their dispute to the ICJ. ▶

Legal principle

The ICJ resolved the dispute by reference to the principle of *uti possidetis*. In its view: 'The maintenance of the territorial status quo in Africa is often seen as the wisest course, to preserve what has been achieved by peoples who have struggled for their independence, and to avoid a disruption which would deprive the continent of the gains achieved by much sacrifice' (at 567).

Self-determination

KEY DEFINITION: Self-determination

The principle of self-determination holds that all peoples have the right to freely determine their political status and to pursue economic, social and cultural development.

KEY INSTRUMENT

Article 1(2) UN Charter

'To develop friendly relations among nations based on respect for the principle of equal rights and self-determination of peoples, and to take other appropriate measures to strengthen universal peace.'

Self-determination was conceived as a political principle but it slowly evolved into an international legal right. Its development owes much to the decolonisation process, which gathered pace in the 1960s.

Forms of self-determination

Decolonisation

KEY INSTRUMENT

UN Colonial Declaration, GA Resolution 1514 (1960)

Paragraph 2: 'All people have the right to self-determination; by virtue of that right they freely determine their political status and freely pursue their economic, social and cultural development . . .'

📖 REVISION NOTE

The Colonial Declaration is a UNGA resolution and so it does not constitute international law per se. However, it quickly achieved CIL status. You should familiarise yourself with the way in which CIL is created. (See Chapter 2.) Moreover, the CIL right to self-determination was further developed by the UN Declaration on Friendly Relations, UNGA Resolution 2625 (1970).

Self-determination was closely associated with the right to found an independent State (*external* self-determination) for the purpose of decolonisation. Its application in this context seemed to be straightforward – the colonised people exercised their right of self-determination by establishing an independent State, which possesses the same territory as the previous colonial unit.

However, independence is not the only option available to colonised peoples seeking to exercise their right of self-determination.

KEY INSTRUMENT

UN Colonial Declaration GA Resolution 1541 (1960)

The right of self-determination for colonised peoples in non-self-governing territories can be exercise by:

(a) the achievement of independent statehood;

(b) by integrating with another territory (e.g. a neighbouring territory); or

(c) by deciding to associate with an established State (usually the previous colonial authority).

! Don't be tempted to . . .

Take care not to confuse General Assembly Resolution 1514 (the Colonial Declaration) with General Assembly Resolution 1541. You may think that I have made a typographical error but I haven't! GA Res. 1541 was adopted by the General Assembly on the day after it adopted GA Res. 1514 – they are two separate resolutions that are connected to the elaboration of the right to self-determination in the colonial context.

□ REVISION NOTE

The above options have acquired CIL status. How would this have occurred? These options were considered and followed during the process of decolonisation, thus satisfying the requirements of *opinio juris* and State practice. (See Chapter 2.)

KEY CASE

The Wall Advisory Opinion (2004) ICJ Rep 136
Concerning: the legality of the construction of a wall dividing Israel and the Palestinian territories
Legal issue: the nature and extent of the right to self-determination in international law ▶

Facts

Israel began to build a wall to divide Israeli and Palestinian territories. It was constructed in such a way that it would incorporate some Palestinian territory into Israel. The UNGA requested an ICJ Advisory Opinion to identify the legal consequences of Israel's actions.

Legal principle

The ICJ decided that the Palestinians constituted a 'people' for the purpose of the exercise of the right of self-determination in international law. Moreover, it held that, by constructing a wall, Israel was impeding the exercise of this right. The ICJ also reaffirmed that the right of self-determination is an obligation *erga omnes*.

 Make your answer stand out

If the Palestinians constitute a unit for the purpose of exercising right to self-determination, are they entitled to establish their own State as a matter of international law? At present, the Palestinian Authorities do not control Palestinian territory effectively; would this undermine any claim to statehood? The criteria for statehood can be relaxed for the purpose of achieving decolonisation. It is widely recognised that the Palestinian situation is an instance of decolonisation. See Crawford (1998).

External self-determination

It is important to remember that the right of self-determination is the right of all peoples. Traditionally, the right of external self-determination was viewed as a 'once and for all' right that was exhausted by the founding of a new State. Moreover, it has achieved the status of a peremptory norm of international law. See the ICJ's decisions in the *Namibia Case*, the *Western Sahara Case*, and the *East Timor Case*.

However, an enduring problem with the application of the right of self-determination has been the difficulty in identifying the unit that is entitled to exercise the right – who constitutes a 'people' for the purpose of exercising right to self-determination? Traditionally, it was assumed that a 'people' should be equated with the population of an independent State (or colonial unit within the context of decolonisation). However, this assumption has been tested in situations when a group has attempted to break away from an existing State in an effort to establish their own State (see below).

Internal self-determination

During the UN era, self-determination has also developed as an internal right – the continuing right to participate in a State's political processes.

KEY INSTRUMENT

Article 1(1), ICCPR (1966)

'All people have the right of self-determination. By virtue of that right they freely determine their political status and freely pursue their economic, social and cultural development.'

The UN Human Rights Committee, which monitors the operation of the ICCPR, stated, in General Comment No. 12 (1984), that: 'State parties should describe the constitutional and political processes which in practice allow for the exercise of this right.'

 Make your answer stand out

Does the right to internal self-determination amount to an entitlement to democratic government? The claim has been advanced by many international lawyers, especially since the end of the Cold War (1989) but the evidence in support of this contention is questionable. Read Franck (1992).

Unilateral secession

KEY CASE

Re Secession of Quebec [1998] 2 SCR 217

Concerning: whether Quebec could secede from Canada

Facts

Quebec wanted to break away from the federal State of Canada in order to establish an independent State. The Canadian government asked the Canadian Supreme Court whether Quebec had a right to unilateral secession under international law pursuant to the right of self-determination.

Legal principle

The court ruled that international law does not recognise a right to unilateral secession. Further, it held that, in general, the right of self-determination is an internal right to be exercised by groups within the confines of a State. It could only be viewed as an external right in exceptional circumstances (e.g. in the context of decolonisation).

International law holds that unilateral secession is neither legal nor illegal. Accordingly, it will not endorse the actions of a group that is trying to break away to establish an independent State (in a non-colonial situation), at least until the entity has established itself effectively.

Make your answer stand out

Should international law adopt such a neutral stance? Are there situations when it should support an attempt to break away from an established State, e.g. the gross and systematic violation of human rights? Was Kosovo's unilateral declaration of independence a valid act of self-determination? See Chapter 4 and Weller (2009).

✎ **EXAM TIP**

You should recognise the way in which the *Quebec Case* is consistent with the reorientation of self-determination away from its external form towards its internal manifestation. The case allows you to reflect on the relationship between external and internal self-determination and the evolution of self-determination in general.

📖 **REVISION NOTE**

The *Quebec Case* is a decision taken by a national court regarding the interpretation of international law. It demonstrates the way in which national legal systems contribute to the development of international law. A good understanding of this authority will help you to illustrate the nature of international law (Chapter 1) and the way that the sources of international law work (Chapter 2).

KEY CASE

Palestine's Claim to Statehood (2012)

Concerning: the creation and recognition of States in international law

Facts

In Resolution 67/19 (2012) the UN General Assembly decided to grant Palestine non-member observer State status at the UN. This prompted speculation about whether Palestine has become a State as a matter of international law.

Legal principle

An entity, which claims to be state, must be able to satisfy the criteria contained in Article 1 of the Montevideo Convention (1933). Palestine maintains a claim to statehood but it cannot satisfy the Montevideo criteria as a result of Israel's ongoing occupation of Palestinian territory. Before 67/19, many international lawyers thought that the Palestinian Authority's lack of effective governmental control over its territory meant that Palestine could not be a State. It is important to remember that, under Article 4(1) of the UN Charter, the UN membership is only open to States. Resolution 67/19 did not admit Palestine to UN membership and so it does not indicate that Palestine is now a State as a matter of international law.

Nevertheless, did those States which voted in favour of Resolution 67/19 collectively recognise the existence of a Palestinian State? Before this resolution, Palestine was recognised as a State by 132 States. Under the constitutive theory of recognition, widespread collective recognition could strengthen an otherwise weak claim to statehood. Accordingly, could the support of 132 States and the applicability of the right of self-determination combine to support Palestine's claim to statehood?

It is worth considering whether the voting record of States in the context of Resolution 67/19 provides sufficient evidence of collective recognition for the State of Palestine: 138 States voted in favour of Resolution 67/19 and nine States voted against it (with 40 States abstaining). Consequently, the resolution reveals a slight increase in the number of States that recognise Palestine's claim to statehood. However, a significant portion of the international community remains non-committal on the question of Palestine's international legal status.

 Make your answer stand out

The circumstances surrounding Resolution 67/19 should prompt you to reflect on the requirements of a claim to statehood, and the relationship between statehood and recognition in international law. The ICJ, in its *Wall Advisory Opinion* (2004), confirmed that the Palestinians are entitled to exercise the right of self-determination in international law. Should the right of self-determination make a difference to the way in which a claim to statehood is treated?

State dissolution

State dissolution occurs where a federal State disintegrates. In such situations, international law may view the constituent republics of the federal State as units entitled to exercise the right of self-determination.

KEY CASE

Dissolution of Yugoslavia (1990–91) (Badinter Committee, Opinion No. 2 (1992) 31 ILM 1498)

Concerning: the creation of new States in the aftermath of the break-up of Yugoslavia
Legal issue: the relationship between self-determination, statehood and recognition in situations of State dissolution

Facts

The federal State of Yugoslavia began to disintegrate. Several of its constituent republics wanted to establish themselves as independent States. The Badinter Arbitration Committee was tasked with advising the EC Conference on Yugoslavia on the legal issues which might arise from this crisis. ▶

> **Legal principle**
>
> The Committee decided that Yugoslavia's constitution gave the republics the right to self-determination which could be exercised through their accession to statehood.

■ Relationship between territory and self-determination

International law prizes stability and it is invariably willing to achieve this by providing for the continuity of existing territorial units. Consequently, in principle, the territorial integrity of existing units takes precedence over any claims of self-determination.

Figure 7.2

Forms of self-determination

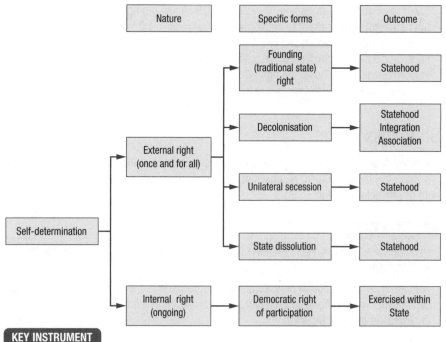

Colonial Declaration GA Resolution 1514 (1960)

Paragraph 6: 'Any attempt aimed at the partial or total disruption of the national unity and the territorial integrity of a country is incompatible with the purposes and principles of the Charter of the United Nations.'

Uti possidetis and self-determination

Uti possidetis has been particularly useful in reinforcing the territorial status quo.

KEY CASE

The Frontier Dispute **(1986) ICJ Rep 554**

Concerning: a sovereignty dispute between Burkina Faso and Mali
Legal issue: that the uti possidetis *principle is not restricted to instances of decolonisation*

Facts

See above.

Legal principle

The ICJ held that *uti possidetis* 'is not a special rule which pertains solely to one specific system of international law. It is a general principle, which is logically connected with the phenomenon of the obtaining of independence, wherever it occurs. Its obvious purpose is to prevent the independence and stability of new states being endangered by fratricidal struggles . . .' (565).

KEY CASE

Dissolution of Yugoslavia **(1990–91) (Badinter Committee, Opinion No. 2 (1992) 31 ILM 1498)**

Concerning: the creation of new States in the aftermath of the break-up of Yugoslavia
Legal issue: the relationship between the principles of self-determination and uti possidetis *in international law*

Facts

See above.

Legal principle

In its second Opinion, the Badinter Committee observed that: '[I]t is well established that, whatever the circumstances, the right to self-determination must not involve changes to existing frontiers at the time of independence (*uti posseditis juris*) except where the states concerned agree otherwise.'

Make your answer stand out

Can the principle of *uti possidetis* be applied in situations of secession? Kosovo was an autonomous province of Yugoslavia. It was not recognised as a federal republic by the 1974 constitution. However, the administrative delimitations of the Yugoslav province of Kosovo became the international boundaries of Kosovo when it acceded to statehood. Some commentators have suggested that this means that *uti possidetis* can apply to cases of secession. See Weller (2009).

📖 **REVISION NOTE**

Whether the exercise of the external right of self-determination will lead to the creation of a new State depends, in part, on how the claim is treated by the international community of States. Accordingly, it is important that you understand the doctrines concerning recognition (which are covered in Chapter 5).

■ Restrictions on territorial claims

Not all territory is open to acquisition. Certain areas are the property of the international community as a whole (*res communis*):

- High Seas (Art. 87, United Nations Convention on the Law of the Sea (UNCLOS) 1982);
- Celestial Bodies of Outer Space (Art. 2, Space Treaty 1967).

The regime developed in relation to Outer Space gave rise to the idea that certain areas should not be subject to sovereign claims; they should instead be viewed as part of our 'common heritage'.

✎ **EXAM TIP**

The Antarctica Treaty (1959) does not prohibit territorial claims concerning Antarctica. Some States have claimed parts of that continent (which have not been accepted by other States). However, developments since 1959 suggest that Antarctica should be viewed as part of our common heritage and is not capable of territorial acquisition. This provides a good example of the way in which international law evolves.

■ Putting it all together

Answer guidelines

See the problem question at the start of the chapter.

Approaching the question

This question involves the following areas:

- the nature of title to territory;
- modes of territorial acquisition;
- self-determination.

Important points to include

Acquisition of Arcadia

- How did O acquire title to Arcadia?
- It appears as though acquisition occurred by occupation.
- Identify and explain the requirements of occupation and whether they were met here.
- O transferred title to R by treaty. Was this a valid cession?
- Was title to Beta included? See *Palmas* and *Clipperton* cases.

The legal basis for X's claim to Beta

- It seems that X has acquired title to B by occupation. But has it satisfied the test established in the *Palmas Case* (continuous and peaceful display of sovereign authority).
- Does the available evidence suggest that X has controlled the territory effectively?
- What kinds of administrative act are sufficient for this purpose? See the *Eastern Greenland Case*.

Self-determination

- Are the Betans entitled to exercise the right of self-determination?
- Discuss external self-determination in the context of decolonisation.

▶

- Identify and discuss the sources of CIL:
  - ☐ Colonial Declaration (1960)
  - ☐ Declaration on Friendly Relations (1970)
  - ☐ Applicable ICJ case law, especially the *Namibia* and *Western Sahara* cases.
- Betans possess the right of self-determination and they can exercise this right.

 Make your answer stand out

- Is the decision to remain part of X a valid exercise of the right to self-determination or is the framing of the choice by X a violation of this right?
- UN Colonial Declaration GA Resolution 1541 (1960) provided that the exercise of the right can take at least three forms – independence, integration and association – and these forms are now recognised as a matter of CIL. The Betans' choice to associate with the former colonial authority is a valid exercise of the right.

READ TO IMPRESS

Crawford, J. (1998) 'State Practice and International Law in relation to Secession', 69 *BYIL* 85.

Franck, T. M. (1992) 'The Emerging Right to Democratic Governance', 86 *AJIL* 46.

Shaw, M. N. (1996) 'The Heritage of States: The Principle of Uti Possidetis Juris Today', 67 *BYIL* 75.

Weller, M. (2009) 'Settling Self-determination Conflicts: Recent Developments', 20 *EJIL* 111.

www.pearsoned.co.uk/lawexpress

 Go online to access more revision support including quizzes to test your knowledge, sample questions with answer guidelines, podcasts you can download, and more!

State responsibility and diplomatic protection

8

Revision checklist

Essential points you should know:

- [ ] Attribution of responsibility to States in international law
- [ ] ILC Articles on State Responsibility (2001)
- [ ] Defences available when responsibility is established
- [ ] Concept and application of diplomatic protection
- [ ] Treatment of aliens in international law
- [ ] Remedies available when State responsibility is established

Topic map

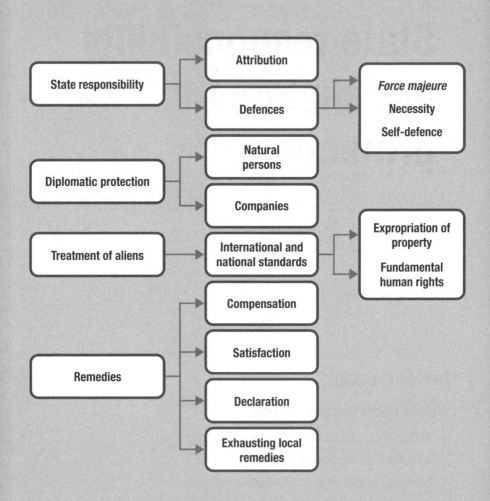

■ Introduction

What are the consequences for States if they breach their international legal obligations? The first part of this chapter focuses on the circumstances in which international law attributes responsibility to States for breaches of international law. Next, the chapter explores the extent to which States can provide diplomatic protection to their nationals when they are within the jurisdiction of another State. The third part considers the duties that a host State owes to the nationals of other States. Finally, the chapter sets out the remedies available in situations when State responsibility is established.

ASSESSMENT ADVICE

State responsibility presupposes a sound knowledge of international law in general. Consequently, students need to know the other areas of international law as well as rules governing State responsibility in order to answer questions on this topic. Questions often take the form of problems and so you should be prepared to apply the relevant law in a given situation. They often focus on the attribution of responsibility for breaches of international law. They also usually raise issues of diplomatic protection and/or the treatment of aliens. It is therefore very important that you learn this topic as a whole.

■ Sample question

Could you answer this question? Below is a typical problem question that could arise on this topic. Guidelines on answering the question are included at the end of this chapter, whilst a sample essay question and guidance on tackling it can be found on the companion website.

PROBLEM QUESTION

Profit Ltd is a company registered in Omega, a developed State. For 40 years it ran a mining operation on Pacifica, a small island State. The mine has been very profitable but has devastated the landscape. In 2010, a revolutionary government took power in Pacifica. In 2011, a group of revolutionary students seized the mine and imprisoned ten of Profit's employees, nationals of another state, Xena, for six months. The employees were eventually released (they complained that they were ill-treated during this period ▶

of detention). Profit protests to the new Pacifican government which said, in response, that the students have ended years of imperialist exploitation, that the mine is now the property of the revolution, and that any complaint should be made to the new revolutionary tribunal which has been established to deal with such complaints. Profit has decided not to complain to the revolutionary tribunal; instead it has asked the governments of Omega and Xena to take action on its behalf. Advise Omega and Xena.

◼ State responsibility

In Resolution 174(II) (1947), the UN General Assembly established the International Law Commission (ILC) with the aim of undertaking studies 'to encourage the progressive development of international law and its codification'. The ILC has been responsible for developing draft Conventions in many areas of international law. In 2001, the ILC finalised and adopted its draft Articles on Responsibility of States for Internationally Wrongful Acts. They were submitted to the UN General Assembly in the same year. Although the ILC did not produce a draft Convention on State Responsibility for Internationally Wrongful Acts, the draft Articles are widely viewed as representative of customary international law in this area of international law.

KEY INSTRUMENT

International Law Commission's Articles on State Responsibility (ASR) (2001)

Article 1: 'Every internationally wrongful act of a State entails the international responsibility of that State.'

The above principle establishes the notion of State liability for internationally wrongful acts. What is an internationally wrongful act? When will a State bear international responsibility for its acts/omissions? What constitutes a State for this purpose?

Attribution

KEY INSTRUMENT

Article 2, ASR (2001)

'There is an internationally wrongful act of a State when conduct consisting of an action or omission:

(a) is attributable to the State under international law; and

(b) constitutes a breach of an international obligation of the State.'

The notions of breach and attribution may be easily established. For example, if a State commences an armed attack on a neighbouring State – in contravention of Article 2(4) UN Charter – responsibility may be attributed. However, this is not always the case (e.g. the controversy concerning the attribution of the 9/11 attacks on the US to Afghanistan).

To what extent should a State be responsible for its failure to prevent a breach of international law?

KEY CASE

Corfu Channel Case (1949) ICJ Rep 4

Concerning: whether Albania was responsible for its failure to act

Facts

Two British warships were damaged by the explosion of mines when they were passing through Albanian waters. The UK claimed that the Albanian government should have alerted the British Navy to the presence of such mines.

Legal principle

The ICJ decided that the mines could not have been laid without the Albanian government's knowledge. It noted that it is 'every State's obligation not to allow knowingly its territory to be used for acts contrary to the rights of other States'. Accordingly, Albania bore international responsibility for the damage suffered.

 Make your answer stand out

In the *Corfu Channel Case* the ICJ endorsed a fault-based (or subjective) approach to State responsibility – it focused on what the Albanian government knew or should have known. However, in the *Caire Claim* (below), it was decided that responsibility was not fault-based; instead, it should be assessed on an objective basis. You should reflect on the implications which flow from the subjective and objective approaches. Should States be able to avoid responsibility in the absence of knowledge? Could it be argued that the result in the *Corfu Channel Case* would have been different if the objective approach had been followed? Articles 1 and 2 ASR (2001) implicitly endorses the objective approach.

What constitutes a State for the purpose of establishing international responsibility? Article 4, ASR (2001) provides that the 'conduct of any State organ shall be considered an act of that State'. Consequently, the acts and/or omissions of any governmental body (including the legislature, executive and judiciary) and, under Article 5 ASR (2001), those agencies which are not *formally* part of the State but which 'exercise elements of governmental authority' shall constitute State conduct for the purpose of establishing State responsibility.

This broad definition of a State for the purpose of State responsibility prevents the avoidance of responsibility for a violation of international law as a result of a State's internal structures of governance. This approach is strengthened by Article 3, ASR (2001), which provides that a State cannot invoke its own national law to avoid international responsibility. The idea is that the State should ensure that its national legal system and its internal system of government enable it to comply with its international legal obligations and thus to avoid international responsibility.

☐ REVISION NOTE

You should remember that international law maintains that national law cannot be invoked to avoid a State's international legal obligations (see Arts. 27 and 46 VCLT (1969)). This is not to say that the offending national law is invalid but it is a good illustration of the 'Fitzmaurice Compromise'. (See Chapter 5.)

✎ EXAM TIP

ASR (2001) is the main reference point on the topic of State responsibility. You should reflect upon its status in international law. It was adopted by the UNGA (GA Res. 56/83 (2001)). However, such resolutions do not create binding international law per se (see Chapter 2). One view is that, because the ILC is comprised of some of the most highly qualified international jurists, its reports can be classified as a subsidiary means for determining international law (under Art. 38(1)(d) ICJ Statute). However, the better view is that it represents (in large part) the CIL concerning State responsibility. Accordingly, while the instrument itself is not a formal source of international law its provisions have codified CIL in many respects. See Crawford (2002).

International law attributes responsibility to States for the acts and omissions of their officials (and those exercising governmental authority). But what if a State's officials exceed their authority? In such situations, to what extent should States be liable for the *ultra vires* conduct of their representatives?

KEY INSTRUMENT

Article 7, ASR (2001)

'The conduct of an organ of a State or of a person or entity empowered to exercise elements of the governmental authority shall be considered an act of the State under international law if the organ, person or entity acts in that capacity, even if it exceeds its authority or contravenes instructions.'

KEY CASE

The Caire Claim (1929) 5 RIAA 516

Concerning: whether Mexico was responsible for the unauthorised actions of its officials

Facts

Two Mexican soldiers tried to extort money from a French national. They took him to local barracks and murdered him.

Legal principle

The French–Mexican Claims Commission decided that international responsibility arose because the officers had: 'acted under cover of their status as officers and used means placed at their disposal on account of that status'.

International law focuses on whether official status has facilitated the unauthorised conduct rather than the scope of an official's legitimate duties. Consequently, responsibility arises from the ability to establish ostensible authority rather than through a test which concentrates on the ability of the State in question to control its officials.

KEY INSTRUMENT

Article 8, ASR (2001)

'The conduct of a person or group of persons shall be considered an act of a State under international law if the person or group of persons is in fact acting on the instructions of, or under the direction or control of, that State in carrying out the conduct.'

Under Article 8, ASR (2001), State responsibility may arise if the conduct which amounts to a breach of international law is directed or controlled by the State. Alternatively, the actions of private individuals may be attributed to the State if they are 'carried out in the absence or default of the official authorities' (Art. 9, ASR (2001)).

KEY CASE

Nicaragua Case (Merits) (1986) ICJ Rep 14

Concerning: whether the US was responsible for paramilitary activities in Nicaragua
Legal issue: the circumstances in which conduct can be attributed to a State for the purpose of establishing international responsibility

Facts

The US government provided logistical, supervisory and financial support to Nicaraguan paramilitaries with the aim of overthrowing the elected government of Nicaragua. ▶

The ICJ had to decide whether this conduct amounted to a breach of international law, and if so, whether it could be attributed to the US.

Legal principle

The ICJ held that for the conduct to be attributable to the US it would need to effectively control the paramilitaries and this could not be established: 'There is no clear evidence of the [US] having actually exercised such degree of control in all fields as to justify treating the [paramilitaries] as acting on its behalf.' Accordingly, the paramilitaries could not be treated as US government agents for the purpose of attributing international responsibility.

! Don't be tempted to . . .

The *Nicaragua Case* is often compared to the decision in *Prosecutor* v *Tadic* (1999) 38 ILM 1518. In *Tadic*, the ICTY Appeals Chamber adopted a test of 'overall control' which meant that planning and supervision would be sufficient to give rise to State responsibility. However, it is important to remember that the ICTY was primarily concerned with establishing individual criminal responsibility rather than State responsibility. You should not assume that the effective control test is no longer good law. The ICJ disapproved of the 'overall control' test in the *Genocide Case (Bosnia-Herzegovina* v *Serbia)* (2007) 46 ILM 188, Para. 406.

KEY INSTRUMENT

Article 10(1), ASR (2001)

'The conduct of an insurrectional movement which becomes the new Government of a State shall be considered an act of that State under international law.'

Article 10, ASR (2001), acknowledges that the conduct of an insurrectional movement can be attributable to the State if that group succeeds in becoming that State's new government. However, if this does not happen then the movement's conduct will be viewed as that of a private group, which would not be attributable to the State.

EXAM TIP

Under Article 11, ASR (2001), conduct may be attributed to a State if it chooses to acknowledge and adopt that conduct as its own. In the *US Diplomatic and Consular Staff in Tehran Case* (1980) ICJ Rep 3, the Iranian leadership issued a decree formally endorsing the seizure of the US Embassy and the detention of its occupants, which was initially carried out by the Revolutionary Guards (a group of private individuals).

Defences

There are a number of well-established defences to State responsibility. The most significant are:

Force majeure – Article 23, ASR (2001)

KEY CASE

The Rainbow Warrior Case **(1987) 26 ILM 1346**

Concerning: State responsibility for a violation of sovereignty
Legal issue: the nature and extent of the defences to State responsibility

Facts

Two security agents acting on behalf of France sank the ship *Rainbow Warrior* in New Zealand's territorial waters. The dispute was settled by a 1985 treaty between France and New Zealand, in which it was agreed that the agents would be detained in an overseas military base for three years. The agents were repatriated before the agreed period had elapsed. France claimed that the reasons for repatriating the agents were beyond its control (*force majeure*).

Legal principle

France's defence of *force majeure* was not established on the facts. Repatriation was justified on medical grounds. However, the Arbitration Panel decided that this did not render the performance of the agreement impossible.

Necessity – Article 25, ASR (2001)

KEY CASE

Gabcikovo-Nagymaros Case **(1997) ICJ Rep 7**

Concerning: liability for the termination of a treaty to construct a dam
Legal issue: the nature and extent of the defences to State responsibility

Facts

Hungary invoked the defence of necessity to justify its decision to abandon construction work on a dam project which would otherwise have resulted in international responsibility.

Legal principle

The ICJ decided that Hungary could not satisfy the requirements of the defence of necessity because there was insufficient evidence that its decision was made in response to a situation of imminent danger to the environment.

Self-defence – Article 21, ASR (2001)

(See Chapter 10.)

✎ EXAM TIP

You should note that defences to State responsibility are quite limited. If defences such as necessity or *force majeure* were easily established, this would weaken international legal rights and obligations substantially. Would this strengthen the arguments of those who claim that international law isn't really law at all (see Chapter 1)? You should reflect on the relationship between treaty breaches and responsibility in this context (see Chapter 3).

📖 REVISION NOTE

Article 26, ASR (2001) provides that State conduct which breaches a peremptory norm of international law (*jus cogens*) is indefensible. You should connect this provision to Article 53 VCLT (1969) and the CIL concerning peremptory norms. (See Chapter 2.)

■ Diplomatic protection

KEY DEFINITION: Diplomatic protection

A State has the right to invoke: 'through diplomatic action or other means of peaceful settlement, of the responsibility of another State for an injury caused by an internationally wrongful act of that State to a natural or legal person that is a national of the former State with a view to the implementation of such responsibility', Article 1, ILC Draft Articles on Diplomatic Protection 2006 (DADP).

States can only exercise the right of diplomatic protection in respect of their nationals (including companies registered in its territory) against another State – Article 3, ILC Draft Articles on Diplomatic Protection 2006 (DADP).

❗ Don't be tempted to . . .

Don't confuse the Articles on State Responsibility (2001) with the Draft Articles on Diplomatic Protection (2006). While both instruments were produced by the International Law Commission they address different areas of international law. The 2006 instrument was adopted by the ILC (58th session (A/61/10)) but it has yet to be adopted by the UNGA. The 2006 instrument reflects CIL in certain respects.

Figure 8.1

Establishing state responsibility for a breach of an international legal obligation

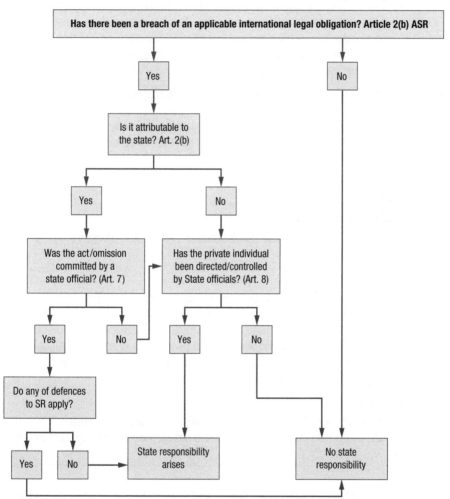

Natural persons

The right to exercise diplomatic protection flows from a State's legal obligation to protect its nationals. As discussed in Chapter 1, traditionally, international law created rights and duties for States (rather than for individuals). It was assumed that States had the right to protect the interests of their own nationals when they came within the jurisdiction of another State. Consequently, a host State would be subject to certain duties regarding the treatment of nationals belonging to another State (see below).

However, problems have arisen in situations where a person is a citizen of more than one State and in cases where he or she has changed nationality (via naturalisation). Further, diplomatic protection can be particularly problematic in situations where a person has dual or multiple nationalities. Which State has the right to exercise diplomatic protection on behalf of such a person? In such a situation, those States which are entitled to exercise diplomatic protection on behalf of their citizen will often join together where a third State exercises jurisdiction over that person.

Difficulties may arise when a dispute occurs between two States and an affected person is a national of both States. In such cases, international law has developed the notion of 'dominant nationality' in order to avoid unfair or inequitable consequences – see the *Merge Claim (US* v *Italy)* (1955) 22 ILR 443. This approach has been endorsed by Article 7 DADP (2006) and it has achieved the status of a CIL rule.

KEY CASE

The Nottebohm Case (1955) ICJ Rep 4

Concerning: whether Liechtenstein could exercise diplomatic protection in favour of one of its citizens

Facts

Nottebohm was a German citizen by birth. He became a naturalised citizen of Liechtenstein in 1939. Consequently, he lost his German citizenship. Nottebohm lived in Guatemala from 1905 to 1940. In 1940, he was arrested and deported to the US where he was interred until 1946. When he was released he was barred from returning to Guatemala and his property in that country was confiscated. Liechtenstein sought to exercise diplomatic protection on his behalf.

Legal principle

The ICJ decided that Nottebohm did not have a genuine link with Liechtenstein. Consequently, it was held that Liechtenstein could not exercise diplomatic protection on his behalf.

Nottebohm has attracted considerable criticism. It has been suggested that the ICJ applied the dominant nationality test, designed for situations where a person possesses more than one nationality, to a situation where the individual had only one nationality.

You should note that Article 4 DADP (2006) does not endorse the genuine link test in respect of the exercise of diplomatic protection on behalf of natural persons.

Companies

Barcelona Traction Case (1970) ICJ Rep 4

Concerning: whether Belgium could exercise diplomatic protection on behalf of its shareholders

Facts

Barcelona Traction Ltd was registered in Canada and so it had Canadian nationality. The company was founded with the aim of developing supplies of electricity in Spain. It was declared insolvent by a Spanish court. Many of its shareholders were Belgian nationals and Belgium brought a claim on behalf of its nationals.

Legal principle

The ICJ decided that Belgium did not have standing to bring a claim against Spain. The company had Canadian nationality and only Canada could invoke the right of diplomatic protection on the facts.

In *Barcelona Traction* the ICJ indicated that, as a general rule, a company would need to have been incorporated and registered in a State for that State to be able to exercise the right of diplomatic protection. In addition, the company would need to maintain 'a close and permanent connection' with the claimant State. This approach was endorsed by Article 9 DADP (2006).

Article 9, DADP (2006)

'. . . when the corporation is controlled by nationals of another state and has no substantial activities in the state of incorporation, and the seats of management and financial control of the corporation are both located in another state, that state shall be regarded as the state of nationality.'

How far is the position adopted in *Barcelona Traction* and developed in Article 9 DADP (2006) from the genuine link test adopted by the ICJ in *Nottebohm*? Why should there be a different standard for natural and artificial legal persons?

Figure 8.2

Diplomatic protection

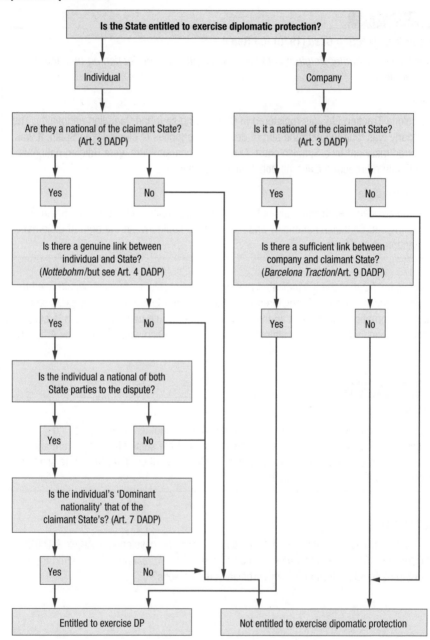

■ Treatment of aliens

The right to exercise diplomatic protection is the right of States. The orthodox position is that a State may choose to extend its protection to its nationals but it is not legally bound to do so (*Barcelona Traction Case* (1970)).

KEY CASE

Mavrommatis Palestine Concession Case (1924) PCIJ Rep Series A, No. 2, 12

Concerning: the exercise of diplomatic protection by Greece

Facts

The Palestinian authorities refused to recognise concessions held by Mavrommatis and obtained from the previous sovereign authority. The Greek government made a claim against the UK (the mandatary power) on his behalf.

Legal principle

The PCIJ noted that: 'It is an elemental principle of international law that a state is entitled to protect its subjects, when injured by acts contrary to international law committed by another state . . . By taking up the case of one of its subjects and by resorting to diplomatic action or international judicial proceedings on his behalf, a state is in reality asserting its own rights – its right to ensure, in the person of subjects, respect for the rules of international law.'

Any remedy awarded by an international tribunal accrues to the State (*Rustomjee* v *The Queen* (1876) 1 QBD 487). However, Article 19(c) DADP (2006) provides that a State should transfer any compensation received as a result of the exercise of diplomatic protection to the affected national or nationals.

    Make your answer stand out

The extent to which the exercise of diplomatic protection is a State right (as opposed to an individual right) is now open to question. *R* (*Abassi*) v *Secretary of State for Foreign Affairs* [2002] EWCA Civ 1598 held that any decision taken by the UK government regarding the exercise of diplomatic protection was subject to judicial review. This position is consistent with Article 19(a) DADP 2006, which provides that States should give due consideration as to the possibility of exercising diplomatic protection.

International and national standards of treatment

The topic of the treatment of aliens is controversial because the applicable standard of treatment in such situations remains contested. Developed States have endorsed an international standard because they are concerned that standards in developing States are not sufficient to protect the interests of their nationals. In contrast, developing States have argued that the treatment of aliens should be determined by national standards because they are anxious to exercise sovereignty over their own resources and to reduce the extent to which those resources are controlled by foreign nationals. These two conflicting approaches have made it difficult to identify the content of international law on particular issues.

Expropriation of property

As noted above, the grounds and consequences of a State's decision to confiscate property belonging to foreign nationals are problematic. It has long been established that a State has the right to expropriate property owned by foreign nationals in certain circumstances (*Certain German Interests in Polish Upper Silesia* (1926) PCIJ Series A, No. 7, 22). The key principles governing the expropriation of property owned by foreign nationals are that:

- expropriation must not be discriminatory; and
- it must be for a public purpose; and
- the foreign nationals must be adequately compensated for their losses.

This area is influenced by two UNGA Resolutions.

KEY INSTRUMENT

Resolution on Permanent Sovereignty over Natural Resources (GA Res. 1803, 1962)

States have the right to expropriate property belonging to foreign nationals. However, Article 4 requires that expropriation satisfies the test of public utility and that appropriate compensation shall be paid in accordance with international law in such cases.

KEY INSTRUMENT

Charter of Economic Rights and Duties of States (GA Res. 3281, 1974)

Any compensation payable should be determined according to the provisions of the expropriating State's municipal laws. Further, the resolution does not restrict lawful expropriation or situations where a public purpose can be demonstrated.

Case law suggests that the 1962 resolution has achieved CIL status whereas the 1974 resolution has not – see *Texaco* v *Libya* (1978) 17 ILM 1.

KEY CASE

BP v *Libya Arbitration* **(1974) 53 ILR 297**

Concerning: a claim of unlawful expropriation of property made against Libya

Facts

Libya issued a decree that permitted the expropriation of property belonging to British companies. Assets belonging to BP were nationalised as a result.

Legal principle

The Arbitrator decided that the expropriation of BP's property in Libya was discriminatory in nature because it: 'was made for purely extraneous political reasons' and thus it amounted to a violation of international law.

KEY CASE

Aminoil v *Kuwait* **(1982) 21 ILM 976**

Concerning: a claim of unlawful expropriation of property made against Kuwait

Facts

Aminoil was an American company which had been granted an oil concession in Kuwait. Kuwait terminated the concession and nationalised the company's assets. It claimed that Kuwait had acted in a discriminatory manner because a Japanese company had not been nationalised.

Legal principle

The tribunal decided that Aminoil had failed to show that its nationality was the material cause of its nationalisation. It held that the expropriation was lawful and that an appropriate amount of compensation had been offered in accordance with international law.

Aminoil confirms that the appropriate standard of compensation in situations of lawful expropriation is that which is determined in accordance with international law. This approach is consistent with Article 4, GA Resolution 1962.

Fundamental human rights

The development of multilateral human rights treaties and advances in CIL has rendered the debate about whether the treatment of aliens should be determined by international or national standards redundant where fundamental human rights are engaged. Examples include:

- right to a fair trial – Article 14 ICCPR (1966);
- prohibition on torture – Torture Convention (1984) and CIL;
- prohibition on racial discrimination – ICERD (1965) and CIL.

You should revise this section alongside Chapters 1, 2 and 6.

The significance of international human rights law in the context of the treatment of aliens is illustrated in the recent ICJ case of *Diallo* (2010).

KEY CASE

Diallo Case (Guinea v DRC) ICJ 30/11/2010 General List No. 103
Concerning: Guinea's claim of diplomatic protection against the DRC

Facts

Diallo, a national of Guinea, was the sole shareholder and director of two companies that were owed money by the DRC government. He commenced legal proceedings against the government to recover the outstanding debts. Diallo was arrested and imprisoned and ultimately expelled from the DRC. Guinea sought to exercise diplomatic protection on his behalf.

Legal principle

The ICJ decided that: (1) Diallo's arrest and detention breached Article 9 ICCPR (which prohibits arbitrary arrest and detention); and (2) that because he had not been given the reasons for his expulsion and in the absence of a tribunal hearing to review grounds for his expulsion the DRC had breached Article 13 ICCPR (which sets out certain procedural guarantees regarding expulsions).

✎ **EXAM TIP**

You should remember that universal human rights (derived either from treaty law or CIL) are often bolstered and elaborated by regional human rights treaties. For example, the right to a fair trial is protected by Article 14 ICCPR, Article 6 ECHR, Article 8 American Convention on Human Rights and Article 7 African Charter. The ICCPR's provisions were supported by the applicable provisions of the African Charter in *Diallo* (2010).

■ Remedies

KEY DEFINITION: Reparations

'Responsibility is the necessary corollary of a right. All rights of an international character involve international responsibility. If the obligation in question is not met, responsibility entails the duty to make reparation.' Huber J in *Spanish Zones of Morocco Claims* (1925) 2 RIAA 615, 641.

KEY CASE

Chorzow Factory Case (Germany v Poland) (1928) PCIJ Series A, No. 17
Concerning: the purpose of reparations when State responsibility is established

Facts

Germany made a claim of State responsibility against Poland arising from the unlawful expropriation of a factory.

Legal principle

The PCIJ noted that: '. . . reparation must, as far as possible, wipe out all the consequences of the illegal act and re-establish the situation which would, in all probability, have existed if that act had not been committed.'

KEY INSTRUMENT

Article 31, ASR (2001)

'The responsible State is under an obligation to make full reparation for the injury caused by the internationally wrongful act. Injury includes any damage, whether material or moral, caused by the internationally wrongful act of a State.'

Reparations can take the form of restitution, compensation and satisfaction or any combination thereof (Art. 34, ASR (2001)). Restitution in kind is often difficult to establish. Consequently, financial compensation and/or satisfaction are more commonly awarded.

Compensation

KEY CASE

'I'm Alone' Case (1933–35) 3 RIAA 1609
Concerning: reparations for the unlawful sinking of a Canadian vessel

Facts

The vessel *I'm Alone* was registered in Canada. It was suspected of smuggling by the US Coast Guard. It was fired upon and sunk unlawfully.

Legal principle

The Arbitration Commission held that the sinking was unlawful and that the US government should apologise to the Canadian government and pay financial compensation in the sum of $25,000.

Satisfaction

Satisfaction refers to situations where the remedy requires the responsible State to issue a public apology accompanied by an undertaking to punish the individuals responsible for the conduct in question and the giving of an assurance that such conduct will not be repeated.

Declarations

In some cases, a tribunal will reach the decision that the mere finding that the defendant State has breached international law is a sufficient remedy. This was the outcome in the *Corfu Channel Case* (1949) and the *Rainbow Warrior Case* (1987) (above).

Exhausting local remedies

Before a State can exercise diplomatic protection on behalf of one of its nationals the individual must have exhausted all legal avenues available to him or her under the national law of the host State.

The justification for this requirement follows from the fact that the host State has *prima facie* jurisdiction (and thus sovereignty) over the affected national. Second, the host State should be given the opportunity to resolve any dispute internally in accordance with its national law (and also through its political processes) before an international dispute arises.

However, there are limits to the local remedies doctrine. Article 15 DADP (2006) identifies a number of exceptions to this approach, including where the local remedies do not provide the opportunity for redress or effective redress.

There is no requirement for an individual to comply with the local remedies doctrine when no effective local remedies exist. Examples would include where local officials are corrupt or unreliable or where they systematically discriminate against claims of foreign nationals.

KEY CASE

Robert E Brown Case (US v UK) (1923) 6 RIAA 120

Concerning: whether local remedies always need to be exhausted

Facts

Brown, a US national, applied for a gold prospecting licence in South Africa. The application was denied despite the fact that Brown was legally entitled to such a licence.

Legal principle

The tribunal decided that there was no need to comply with the local remedies doctrine. It noted that: 'A claimant in a foreign state is not required to exhaust justice in such a State where there is no justice to exhaust.'

ELSI Case (US v *Italy)* **(1989) ICJ Rep 15**

Concerning: the scope of the local remedies doctrine

Facts

The case concerned alleged injuries suffered by US companies in Italy.

Legal principle

The ICJ decided that the local remedies doctrine will be satisfied if the claimant State has exhausted all available local remedies in substance as apparent from all the circumstances of the case and according to the principle of good faith.

■ Putting it all together

Answer guidelines

See the problem question at the start of the chapter.

Approaching the question

The question involves the following topics:

- state responsibility;
- exercise of the right of diplomatic protection;
- treatment of aliens.

Important points to include

- A State is responsible for its breaches of international law (Art. 1 ASR 2001).
- Discuss the attribution of responsibility in general terms (Art. 2 ASR 2001).
- Is Pacifica responsible for the actions of the revolutionary students who seized Profit's premises and detained its employees?
    - ☐ Are the students State officials? Do they exercise governmental authority? Article 4 and 5 ASR 2001. If the students are a group of private individuals, Pacifica will not be responsible for their actions. However, you should consider the exceptions to this principle.

▶

- ☐ Are students acting on the instructions of the new Pacifican government or are they under its control (Art. 8 ASR 2001)? Discuss the effective control test (*Nicaragua Case*).
- ☐ Do the students constitute an insurrectional movement that subsequently became the new government of Pacifica? Discuss Article 10 ASR 2001.
- ☐ Did the government adopt the students' actions as its own under Article 11 ASR 2001 (*Tehran Case*)?

■ Profit Ltd is a national of Omega and so that State can choose to exercise diplomatic protection on its behalf. However, Omega should satisfy itself that there is a sufficient link between itself and the company. See *Barcelona Traction Case* (1970) and Article 9 DADP 2006.

■ If Omega is satisfied, it could bring a claim against Pacific with regard to the expropriation of the company's property.

■ Was the expropriation lawful as a matter of international law?

- ☐ Was it discriminatory? See *BP* v *Libya* (1974).
- ☐ Was it for a public purpose? See GA Res. 1803 (1962).
- ☐ Was Profit Ltd offered an appropriate level of compensation? See GA Res. 1803 (1962).

■ Profit's employees were nationals of Xena. It could choose to make a claim of diplomatic protection on their behalf.

■ Has Pacifica satisfied the requirements of international law regarding the treatment of aliens?

- ☐ Detentions appear to violate Article 14 ICCPR (1966).
- ☐ Complaints of ill-treatment may give rise to claims under the Torture Convention (1984).
- ☐ If Pacifica has not ratified these multilateral treaties, is there any applicable CIL?

✓ **Make your answer stand out**

- ■ To bring a claim before an international tribunal would Omega and Xena need to satisfy the local remedies doctrine? See the *Brown Case* (1923).
- ■ How could Omega and Xena make a claim of State responsibility? Would it matter if Pacifica was unwilling to defend itself in ICJ proceedings?

READ TO IMPRESS

Crawford, J. (2002) *The International Law Commission's Draft Articles on State Responsibility: Introduction, Text and Commentaries.* Cambridge University Press.

Crawford, J. and Olleson, S. (2010) 'The Nature and Forms of International Responsibility', in M. D. Evans, *International Law*, 3rd edn. Oxford University Press.

International Law Commission, Draft Articles on Diplomatic Protection and Commentaries: http://untreaty.un.org/ilc/texts/instruments/english/commentaries/9_8_2006.pdf

International Law Commission, Draft Articles on State Responsibility and Commentaries: http://untreaty.un.org/ilc/texts/instruments/english/commentaries/9_6_2001.pdf

www.pearsoned.co.uk/lawexpress

Go online to access more revision support including quizzes to test your knowledge, sample questions with answer guidelines, podcasts you can download, and more!

Judicial dispute resolution

9

Revision checklist

Essential points you should know:

- [ ] Ways in which international legal disputes can be resolved
- [ ] Function of the ICJ
- [ ] ICJ's jurisdiction in contentious cases
- [ ] Significance of ICJ decisions
- [ ] ICJ's advisory jurisdiction

■ Topic map

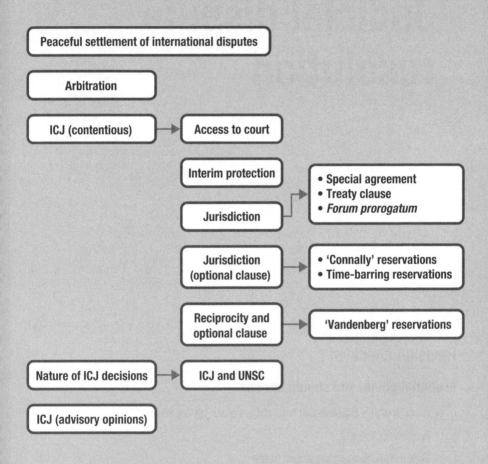

Peaceful settlement of international disputes

Arbitration

ICJ (contentious) → Access to court

Interim protection

Jurisdiction → • Special agreement
• Treaty clause
• *Forum prorogatum*

Jurisdiction (optional clause) → • 'Connally' reservations
• Time-barring reservations

Reciprocity and optional clause → 'Vandenberg' reservations

Nature of ICJ decisions → ICJ and UNSC

ICJ (advisory opinions)

A printable version of this topic map is available from **www.pearsoned.co.uk /lawexpress**

◼ Introduction

No international court is endowed with compulsory jurisdiction to resolve international legal disputes between States. Nevertheless, modern international law is committed to the resolution of international disputes by peaceful means. The international legal system has developed a number of ways of resolving such disputes by judicial settlement. There has been a tremendous growth in the number of judicial bodies which have jurisdiction to decide disputes about international law. However, many of them involve individuals making claims against their own State (e.g. the ECHR) or claims against individuals (e.g. the ICC). These judicial bodies are important institutions for the creation and enforcement of international law (see Chapter 1). However, as this book focuses primarily on the inter-State legal system, this chapter will concentrate on the resolution of inter-State disputes by judicial means.

ASSESSMENT ADVICE

Assessment questions often take the form of essay questions that invite students to consider how disputes are resolved by recourse to judicial bodies in general or by reference to a particular body (e.g. the ICJ). Questions are typically formulated in broad terms so that students will need to demonstrate their understanding of how a given judicial body works. In addition, students may be asked to weigh up the relative strengths and weaknesses of a particular court. To answer such questions you will need to acquire an appreciation of relevant judicial decisions and the international instruments (e.g. the UN Charter and the ICJ Statute) that empower the tribunal in issue.

◼ Sample question

Could you answer this question? Below is a typical essay question that could arise on this topic. Guidelines on answering the question are included at the end of this chapter, whilst a sample problem question and guidance on tackling it can be found on the companion website.

ESSAY QUESTION

'While [the ICJ] may not be such a World Court as idealists might like to envisage, in its present structure and operation it remains a real force for peaceful settlement of disputes, and the furthest extension of judicial power to the affairs of States that is likely to be acceptable to the members of the present-day international community' (Thirlway, 'The International Court of Justice', in M. Evans, *International Law* (2003) 587). Discuss.

Peaceful settlement of international disputes

Article 2(3), UN Charter

All members shall settle their international disputes by peaceful means in such a manner that international peace and security and justice are not endangered.

Article 33, UN Charter

'The parties to any dispute, the continuance of which is likely to endanger the maintenance of international peace and security, shall, first of all, seek a solution by negotiation, enquiry, mediation, conciliation, arbitration, judicial settlement, resort to regional agencies or arrangements, or other peaceful means of their own choice.'

- *Negotiation* – this involves direct contact between the parties to a dispute.
- *Mediation and 'Good Offices'* – this involves using a neutral third party as a negotiator.
- *Commissions of inquiry* – this is where an independent body is used to establish the factual basis of a particular dispute. Its findings may provide the foundations for a negotiated settlement.
- *Conciliation* – where an independent body is engaged to investigate the dispute and to provide a report containing recommendations targeted to resolving the dispute. However, such reports are not legally binding on the parties.

The above methods of dispute resolution do not necessarily involve international law and so you do not need to learn about them in detail.

Arbitration

'a procedure for the settlement of disputes between states by a binding award on the basis of law and as a result of an undertaking voluntarily accepted.' ILC Rep (1953).

Arbitration has three important features in the context of international law:

- it is concerned with the resolution of an international dispute by reference to the rights and duties of the parties as a matter of international law;

- the decisions of arbitral bodies are legally binding on the parties to the dispute;
- the parties are allowed to select the person or persons that will be given the job of deciding the particular dispute in question.

The use of arbitration as a means of resolving international legal disputes has a long history. Examples include:

- *Alabama Arbitration* (1872) (see Chapter 5);
- *Island of Palmas Case* (1928) (see Chapter 7);
- *Rainbow Warrior Case* (1987) (see Chapter 8).

The success of arbitration stems largely from its consensual nature (as opposed to being compulsory); its ad hoc quality and the fact that it allows parties to select the decision makers between themselves.

> ✎ **EXAM TIP**
>
> It is important to recognise that arbitration is not restricted only to States. Non-State actors have also used arbitration to resolve international legal disputes. See *Texaco* v *Libya* (1978) 17 ILM 1.

> **!** Don't be tempted to . . .
>
> 'Arbitration' can mean the resolution of any dispute by a third party and so it does not necessarily involve the application of law. You should not confuse this general meaning with the more specific meaning attributed to arbitration in international law.

ICJ and PCIJ

The ICJ is the current guardian of international law. The first 'World Court' was the Permanent Court of International Justice (PCIJ), which was established in 1920 under the auspices of the League of Nations (1919). Through its judgments the PCIJ was responsible for delivering some of the most important pronouncements on international law (e.g. the *Lotus Case* (1927) (see Chapters 1 and 6)). It was superseded by the ICJ, which was created by the ICJ Statute (1945).

> **KEY INSTRUMENT**
>
> **Article 92, UN Charter**
>
> 'The [ICJ] shall be the principal judicial organ of the United Nations. It shall function in accordance with the annexed Statute, which is based upon the Statute of the [PCIJ] and forms an integral part of the present Charter.'

The function of the World Court remains the same. Consequently, the decisions of the PCIJ and the ICJ have the same authority in international law.

📖 **REVISION NOTE**

What is the status of ICJ decisions as a matter of international law? Do they constitute sources of international law? See Article 38(1), ICJ Statute (which is covered in Chapter 2).

■ ICJ contentious cases

Access to the Court

Article 35, ICJ Statute provides that only States have access to court (subject to special provisions). Under Article 93 (1), UN Charter, all member States are parties to the ICJ Statute.

Before the ICJ will admit a case, it must be satisfied that:

- the dispute is a legal dispute (i.e. capable of being settled by the application of principles and rules of international law); and
- it has jurisdiction to decide the particular dispute in question.

KEY CASE

Nicaragua Case (Jurisdiction) **(1984) ICJ Rep 169**

Concerning: responsibility for paramilitary activities in Nicaragua
Legal issue: the exercise of jurisdiction by the ICJ

Facts

This case concerned the scope of the prohibition on the use of force in international law. A declaration made by the US restricted the ICJ's jurisdiction to decide the case (the declaration stated that treaty law was inapplicable to the dispute). The ICJ had to decide whether it had jurisdiction to hear the case.

Legal principle

The ICJ held that it had jurisdiction and that the dispute could be decided by reference to the applicable CIL.

Interim protection measures

Article 41, ICJ Statute

(1) The Court shall have the power to indicate, if it considers that circumstances so require, any provisional measures which ought to be taken to preserve the respective rights of either party.

(2) Pending the final decision, notice of the measures suggested shall forthwith be given to the parties and to the Security Council.

La Grand (Provisional Measures) (1999) ICJ Rep 9

Concerning: the significance of provisional measures

Facts

La Grand was convicted of murder in the US in 1982. He was sentenced to death. It was subsequently discovered that he was a German national and that he should have been informed of his right to consular access under Article 36(1)(b) Vienna Convention on Consular Relations (1963). Germany instituted ICJ proceedings. It made a request for provisional measures pending determination of the merits of the case.

Legal principle

The ICJ held that the purpose of provisional measures was to allow the Court to maintain the status quo until the case could be determined. It confirmed that the ICJ's decisions regarding provisional measures are legally binding as a matter of international law.

However, the US government was of the view that provisional measures were not binding and so La Grand's execution was not stayed. The ICJ reaffirmed the position that its decisions concerning provisional measures are legally binding when it reached a decision on the merits of the case ((2003) ICJ Rep 3). Moreover, it found that the US had breached the 1963 Convention.

Jurisdiction

Article 36(1), ICJ Statute

The jurisdiction of the Court comprises all cases which the parties refer to it and all matters specially provided for in the [UN] Charter or in treaties and conventions in force.

Article 36(1) ICJ Statute emphasises the requirement that a State has consented to the resolution of a particular legal dispute by judicial means. Consent may be expressed in a number of ways:

Special agreement (*compromis*)

KEY CASE

Maritime Delimitation and Territorial Questions (Jurisdiction) Case (1994) ICJ Rep 112

Concerning: whether the ICJ had jurisdiction to decide a sovereignty dispute
Legal issue: how the ICJ acquires jurisdiction to determine an international legal dispute

Facts

Qatar and Bahrain were in dispute about certain maritime and territorial issues. They sought to enter into an agreement so that the dispute could be referred to the ICJ. No *compromis* was agreed. However, the parties decided that if agreement could not be reached by May 1991 then the matter could be referred to the ICJ. This position was confirmed in the minutes of a meeting held in December 1990 and signed by the foreign ministers of Qatar and Bahrain. No settlement was reached by the material date and Qatar instituted legal proceedings.

Legal principle

The ICJ decided that the minutes of the December 1990 meeting constituted an international agreement which could give rise to ICJ jurisdiction.

Jurisdictional clause in a treaty

KEY CASE

Territorial Dispute (Libya v *Chad)* (1994) ICJ Rep 6

Concerning: a boundary dispute between neighbouring States
Legal issue: how the ICJ can acquire jurisdiction through a jurisdictional clause in a treaty

Facts

The dispute centred on the question of whether a 1955 treaty concluded between Libya and France (the colonial power then responsible for Chad's territory) established the international boundary between the two territories. The treaty contained a clause giving the ICJ jurisdiction in the event of a dispute.

Legal principle

The ICJ observed that the 1955 treaty: 'clearly conveys the intention of the parties to reach a definitive settlement of the question of their common frontiers' (Para. 51).

Forum prorogatum

Forum prorogatum arises where consent is identifiable from the conduct of a respondent State.

KEY CASE

Certain Questions of Mutual Assistance (Djibouti v France) (2008) ICJ Rep 544

Concerning: the basis for the ICJ jurisdiction in relation to a treaty dispute

Facts

Djibouti alleged that France had failed to comply with obligations agreed in a bilateral treaty between the two States. Djibouti commenced legal proceedings before the ICJ. In a letter written to the ICJ, France agreed that the Court had jurisdiction to hear the case.

Legal principle

The ICJ observed that a claim of *forum prorogatum* can arise 'when a respondent State has, through its conduct before the Court or in relation to the applicant party, acted in such a way as to have consented to the jurisdiction of the Court . . .'

Jurisdiction via the optional clause

KEY INSTRUMENT

Article 36(2), ICJ Statute

The state parties to the present Statute may at any time declare that they recognize as *compulsory ipso facto* and without special agreement, in relation to any other state accepting the same obligation, the jurisdiction of the Court in all legal disputes concerning:

(a) the interpretation of a treaty;

(b) any question of international law;

(c) the existence of any fact which, if established, would constitute a breach of an international obligation;

(d) the nature or extent of the reparation to be made for the breach of an international obligation.

This provision permits compulsory jurisdiction in situations where a State party has made a declaration under Article 36(2). Accordingly, compulsory jurisdiction exists in

Figure 9.1

ICJ jurisdiction

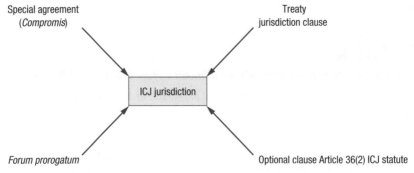

relation to the matters contained in Article 36(2). However, there is no obligation on the State to make such a declaration and therefore jurisdiction under this provision is not compulsory.

While a significant number of States have made such declarations a number of States have withdrawn and the UK remains the only permanent member of the UNSC that has made a current declaration under the optional clause.

Although an optional clause declaration amounts to a unilateral act it only has significance bilaterally. Consequently, it can only have legal effect in a situation where the other party to the dispute has also made such declaration pursuant to Article 36(2).

KEY CASE

Rights of Passage Case (Preliminary Objections) **(1957) ICJ Rep 125**
Concerning: jurisdiction arising out of the optional clause

Facts

Portugal claimed a local CIL rule had been created that allowed it to reach three Portuguese territorial enclaves that were surrounded by territory belonging to India. Portugal deposited its declaration with the UN Secretary General. It instituted legal proceedings against India three days later. At that time, India did not know that Portugal had joined the optional system. It argued that a State could not issue legal proceedings under the optional clause until other States within the optional system had been notified of its declaration.

Legal principle

The ICJ decided that it was open to Portugal to initiate legal proceedings by the optional clause as soon as its declaration was deposited with the UN Secretary-General.

States that have made declarations under the optional system have made reservations in respect of their declarations. The most popular are as follows.

'Connally' reservations

This reservation was developed by the US. It provided that the US would not be bound to accept the court jurisdiction in matters essentially within the domestic jurisdiction of the US, as determined by the US government. Such reservations are now widely made by States. See *Norwegian Loans Case (France v Norway)* (1957) ICJ Rep 9 (below).

Time-barring reservations

For example, the UK has excluded proceedings brought within 12 months of depositing a declaration under the optional clause. This reservation is designed to prevent States from being ambushed by unforeseeable litigation in the ICJ of the kind witnessed in the *Rights of Passage Case* (1957), above. Such a reservation was upheld in the *Case Concerning the Legality of the Use of Force (Yugoslavia v UK) (Provisional Measures)* (1999) ICJ Rep 916.

Reservations relating to particular States

For example, the UK has excluded jurisdiction under the optional clause regarding disputes with Commonwealth States. The idea behind such reservations is that States belonging to a particular organisation may have ways of resolving disputes between member States that are more conciliatory than through ICJ litigation.

Reciprocity and the optional clause

KEY INSTRUMENT

Article 36(3), ICJ Statute

The declarations referred to [in 36(2)] may be made unconditionally or on condition of reciprocity on the part of several or certain states, or for a certain time.

Reciprocity has two effects:

1   the optional clause applies only between participating States;
2   the ICJ exercises jurisdiction only over those disputes where the parties' declarations coincide.

A State may therefore rely on another State's reservation.

KEY CASE

Norwegian Loans Case (1957) ICJ Rep 9

Concerning: a claim brought by France on behalf of French nationals who held bonds in Norwegian companies

Facts

France brought legal proceedings against Norway under the optional clause. Norway argued that France was unable to invoke the optional clause as the basis for the ICJ's jurisdiction because of France's own reservation to Article 36(2). The French reservation declared that the optional clause would not apply to matters that were essentially within France's domestic jurisdiction (as determined by the French government). Norway had not made any such reservation to the optional clause.

Legal principle

The ICJ decided that, under Article 36(3), as the dispute was concerned with matters within Norway's domestic jurisdiction, the principle of reciprocity barred its jurisdiction in the case. Accordingly, the ICJ declined jurisdiction.

'Vandenberg' reservations

A 'Vandenberg' reservation holds that jurisdiction arising out of the operation of the optional clause will *only* be effective in relation to a particular multilateral treaty if all the parties to the dispute are parties to the case *and* to the multilateral treaty in question.

KEY CASE

Nicaragua Case (Jurisdiction) (1984) ICJ Rep 169

Concerning: responsibility for paramilitary activities in Nicaragua
Legal issue: the way in which a reservation can restrict the ICJ's jurisdiction to determine an international legal dispute

Facts

The US made a 'Vandenberg' reservation to Article 36(2), ICJ Statute. It claimed that Costa Rica and El Salvador were also in dispute with Nicaragua, and that they were parties to the UN Charter. However, the US noted that these States were not parties to the *Nicaragua Case* before the ICJ. Accordingly, the US argued that the reservation was effective and the ICJ lacked jurisdiction to hear the case.

Legal principle

The ICJ accepted that the reservation was effective. However, it decided that the reservation was only effective in so far as it excluded applicable treaty law. Accordingly, the UN Charter could not be relied upon to resolve the dispute but the ICJ still had jurisdiction to decide the dispute by reference to CIL.

■ Nature of ICJ decisions

Article 94(1), UN Charter provides that all member States are under an obligation to comply with the ICJ's decisions. Further, Article 94(2) provides that if a State party fails to comply with such a decision the other party to the case can submit the matter to UNSC. UNSC may then take such steps as it considers appropriate in order to enforce the judgment.

ICJ judgments are binding on the parties but the court does *not* follow the doctrine of *stare decisis* (judicial precedent) (Art. 59, ICJ Statute). However, the ICJ typically follows the legal rules and principles established in previous ICJ cases. Clearly, this is a sensible approach since it promotes consistent decision making and legal certainty.

> **📖 REVISION NOTE**
>
> You should remember that while ICJ decisions are binding on the parties they are not a source of international law per se. Article 38(1)(d) stipulates that they are a subsidiary means for the determination of international law. (See Chapter 2.)

Figure 9.2

Establishing ICJ jurisdiction via the optional clause

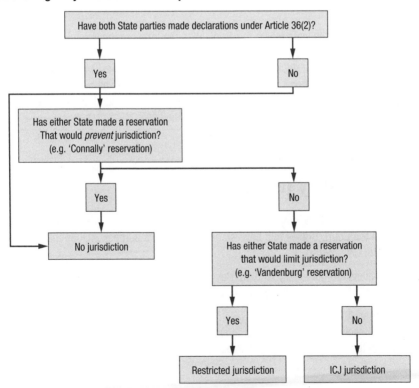

ICJ and UNSC

The US refused to accept the ICJ's decision in the *Nicaragua Case* (1986). Nicaragua complained to the UNSC pursuant to Article 94(2). However, the US exercised its veto and thus it stopped the UNSC from taking any steps to enforce the judgment.

KEY CASE

Lockerbie Case (Libya v *US/UK)* **(Provisional Measures) (1992) ICJ Rep 114**

Concerning: the interpretation and application of the 1971 Montréal Convention arising from the aerial incident at Lockerbie
Legal issue: whether the ICJ has the power to review UNSC decisions

Facts

Libya sought to challenge the legality of sanctions imposed on it by UNSC under SC Resolution 748 (1992) for failing to hand over those suspected of being responsible for the 'Lockerbie Bomb'. It claimed that the ICJ had jurisdiction to review the resolution and, in particular, that the ICJ could order provisional measures given that there was a risk that the sanctions would cause Libya imminent and irreparable damage.

Legal principle

The ICJ decided that Libya's failure to comply with the terms of the resolution was (in effect) self-inflicted and its behaviour was likely to cause harm to US and UK nationals. The ICJ did not decide whether it had the power to review the legality of a UNSC resolution or whether it was bound to accept the resolution as binding upon it. Nevertheless, it decided to take note of the resolution when considering the issue of whether provisional measures were appropriate in the case.

ICJ advisory jurisdiction

Articles 65–68, ICJ Statute, empower a body duly authorised by the UN to seek an Advisory Opinion from the Court. Bodies that have standing for such a purpose include the UNGA and UNSC (Art. 96, UN Charter).

Advisory Opinions are not legally binding. However, if an Advisory Opinion affects the rights and obligations of States they are generally acted upon

A request for an Advisory Opinion must give rise to a legal question because the ICJ is only authorised to resolve legal disputes and to consider legal matters. However, often requests manifest both legal and political dimensions.

The Nuclear Weapons Opinion (1996) ICJ Rep 226

Concerning: the legality of the threat or use of nuclear weapons

Facts

By GA Resolution 49/75K (1994), UNGA requested an Advisory Opinion regarding the following question: 'Is the threat or use of nuclear weapons in any circumstances permitted by international law?'

Legal principle

The ICJ observed that 'It is undoubtedly because a great many rules of humanitarian law applicable in armed conflict are so fundamental to the respect of the human person and "elementary considerations of humanity" . . . Further these fundamental rules are to be observed by all States whether or not they have ratified the conventions that contain them, because they constitute intransgressible principles of international customary law' (at Para. 79).

However, it decided that it did 'not have sufficient elements to enable it to conclude with certainty that the use of nuclear weapons would necessarily be at variance with the principles and rules applicable in armed conflicts in any circumstances' (at Para. 95).

 Make your answer stand out

The *Nuclear Weapons Case* demonstrates the overt political dimension of some requests for Advisory Opinions. Are the issues considered by the ICJ in this case matters for international law to resolve? How could the ICJ reach the conclusion that the latent threat or use of nuclear weapons would be illegal given that all the UNSC permanent members possessed such weapons and in the light of the recent history of the Cold War? Alternatively, how could the ICJ rule that the use or threat to use nuclear weapons was lawful given that the use of such weapons would violate the right to life of potentially millions of innocent people? Read Koskenniemi (1997).

The Wall Opinion (2004) ICJ Rep 136

Concerning: the legality of the construction of a wall dividing Israel and the Palestinian territories
Legal issue: the circumstances in which UNGA can request an Advisory Opinion

Facts

Israel began to build a wall to divide Israeli and Palestinian territories. The wall was constructed in such a way that it would incorporate some Palestinian territory into ▶

Israel. UNGA requested an Advisory Opinion to identify the legal consequences of Israel's actions. Israel argued that UNGA did not have the authority to request an Advisory Opinion.

Legal principle

Article 12, UN Charter prevents UNGA from making 'recommendations' concerning a dispute with which the UNSC was seized by virtue of its Chapter VII powers. However, the ICJ decided that this provision did not stop UNGA from requesting an Advisory Opinion on legal issues relating to the dispute.

KEY CASE

The Kosovo Opinion (2010) ICJ 22/07/2010 General List No. 141

Concerning: the validity of Kosovo's declaration of independence as a matter of international law

Facts

In 1999 NATO embarked on a military campaign to end FRY/Serbia's armed repression of the province of Kosovo. UNSC subsequently placed Kosovo under international administration (although it confirmed that Kosovo notionally remained part of FRY/Serbia). In 2008, representatives of Kosovo made a unilateral declaration of independence. UNGA subsequently requested an Advisory Opinion on the following question: 'Is the unilateral declaration of independence by the Provisional Institutions of Self-Government of Kosovo in accordance with international law?'

Legal principle

The ICJ decided that the question asked 'whether or not the applicable international law prohibited the declaration of independence' (at Para. 56). It decided that the declaration of independence did not violate international law.

 Make your answer stand out

Compare and contrast the ICJ's Advisory Opinions in the *Nuclear Weapons Case* and the *Kosovo Case*. Could you use these decisions to question the viewpoint that every international situation is capable of being determined by international law? Would it have been better if the ICJ had declined jurisdiction in these cases?

■ Putting it all together

Answer guidelines

See the essay question at the start of the chapter.

Approaching the question

This question concerns the following areas:

■ the ICJ's function and purpose;

■ the ICJ's jurisdiction;

■ relevant ICJ case law;

■ nature of international law.

Important points to include

■ This question invites you to reflect upon the effectiveness of the ICJ.

■ Mandate of the ICJ and the basis for its jurisdiction.

■ Role and function of State consent and the way it provide the ICJ with jurisdiction to decide international legal disputes.

■ Analyse Article 36(1), ICJ Statute and the various ways by which the ICJ can establish jurisdiction (see Art. 36(2) and the attendant case law).

■ Consider whether Advisory Opinions have assisted in the resolution of international disputes. While there are Advisory Opinions that have promoted international peace and stability (e.g. the *Namibia Opinion* (1971)), they have not always had positive effects (see *Western Sahara Opinion* (1975), *Nuclear Weapons Case* (1996), the *Wall Opinion* (2004), and the *Kosovo Opinion* (2010)).

■ Reflect upon the body of ICJ decisions in order to assess whether it satisfies its terms of reference.

■ Show awareness of the difficult balance the ICJ has to maintain between legal and political considerations and whether it has been successful in this regard. ▶

Make your answer stand out

- Assess the ICJ comparatively by drawing upon other international tribunals and quasi-judicial bodies in order to determine whether a different model would be more successful.

- Examine the nature of international law itself, e.g. if international law is based on the consent model then this will have major consequences for the role and function of any World Court.

READ TO IMPRESS

Collier, J. and Lowe, V. (1999) *The Settlement of Disputes in International Law*. Oxford University Press.

Koskenniemi, M. (1997) 'Faith, Identity, and the Killing of the Innocent: International Lawyers and Nuclear Weapons', 10 *LJIL* 137.

Oda, S. (2000) 'The Compulsory Jurisdiction of the International Court of Justice: A Myth?', 49 *ICLQ* 251.

Thirlway, H. W. A. (2010) 'The International Court of Justice', in M. Evans, *International Law*, 3rd edn.Oxford University Press.

www.pearsoned.co.uk/lawexpress

 Go online to access more revision support including quizzes to test your knowledge, sample questions with answer guidelines, podcasts you can download, and more!

10

Use of force

Revision checklist

Essential points you should know:

☐ UN Charter and the prohibition on the use of force

☐ 'Aggression' and the CIL rules prohibiting the use of force

☐ Use of force authorised by the UN Security Council

☐ Right of self-defence (unilateral and collective)

☐ Humanitarian intervention

■ Topic map

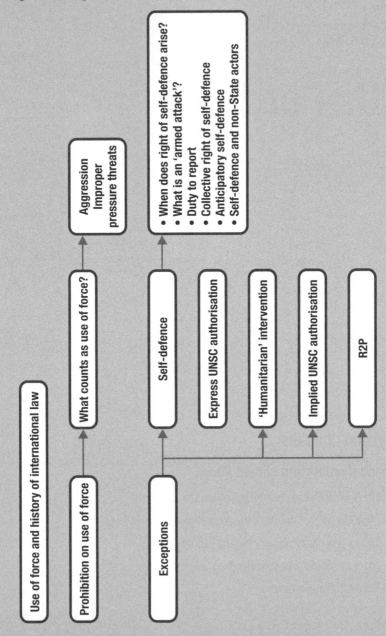

■ Introduction

The UN is committed to the peaceful resolution of international disputes and modern international law advances this commitment by prohibiting States from using force in the conduct of their international relations. The prohibition on the use of force is a fundamental principle of modern international law. However, States have challenged its scope and exceptions to the prohibition do exist. As a result, this area of international law remains highly controversial. Nevertheless, it should be acknowledged that the UNSC plays a vital role in maintaining international peace and security (and it can authorise the use of force to protect the same).

ASSESSMENT ADVICE

Problem questions

Problem questions typically cover a number of related areas of international law and so you need to be able to combine your knowledge of the use of force with your knowledge of other topics (e.g. State responsibility and dispute resolution). It is conceivable that one State may allege a breach of the prohibition on the use of force while another State may claim that it was acting in self-defence. Consequently, it is important that you appreciate how different international rights and obligations relate to each other.

Essay questions

Essay questions often ask students to compare different regimes concerning the use of force (e.g. Art. 2(4) UN Charter and the UNGA Resolution on the Definition of Aggression (1974)); or to analyse a particular issue for the use of force/self-defence (e.g. terrorism) or in a particular context (e.g. Israel/Palestine); or to analyse tensions that exist in this area of law (e.g. prohibition/self-defence or non-intervention/humanitarian intervention). To answer these questions you will need to have a good understanding of the applicable international instruments and the key cases mentioned in this chapter.

■ Sample question

Could you answer this question? Below is a typical essay question that could arise on this topic. Guidelines on answering the question are included at the end of this chapter, whilst a sample problem question and guidance on tackling it can be found on the companion website.

ESSAY QUESTION

Are there any circumstances in which the use of force may still be lawful in modern international law?

■ Use of force and the history of international law

The influence of the natural law tradition in the early international law (see Chapter 1) was evident in the 'just war' theory. In the seventeenth century, it was claimed that war fulfilled a quasi-judicial function. International lawyers argued that it could be waged only if there was 'just cause' (e.g. in self-defence or as a means of securing reparations for injuries suffered or to punish material breaches of international law). However, by the nineteenth century, warfare was considered to be a legitimate instrument for States to use in the conduct of their international affairs. The idea that a State had to have just cause to use force was abandoned, a shift that favoured those States which possessed the greatest military strength.

The Kellogg–Briand Pact (1928), a treaty agreed under the auspices of the League of Nations (1919), condemned the resort to war as an instrument for the advancement of national policy and as a means of resolving international controversies. However, certain States continued to use force in order to advance their national interests and the integrity of the 1928 treaty was ultimately shattered by the Second World War.

! Don't be tempted to . . .

Don't confuse the law regulating the prohibition on the use of force by States and its exceptions (*jus ad bellum*) with the international law of armed conflict (*jus in bello*). Although there is some overlap between the two areas (e.g. the doctrine of humanitarian intervention, as discussed below) they are distinct topics. The current chapter focuses on *jus ad bellum*.

■ Prohibition on the use of force in modern international law

The UN Charter sought to prohibit the use of force and acts of **aggression** by States. According to Article 1, UN Charter, the purposes of the UN include:

> to maintain international peace and security . . .to take effective collective measures for the prevention and removal of threats to the peace, and for the suppression of acts of aggression . . .

KEY INSTRUMENT

Prohibition on use of force

Article 2(4), UN Charter: 'All Members shall refrain in their international relations from the threat or use of force against the territorial integrity or political independence of any State, or in any other manner inconsistent with the Purposes of the United Nations.'

Principle 1, UN Declaration on the Principles of International Law concerning Friendly Relations, UNGA Resolution 2625, (1970): 'Every State has the duty to refrain in its international relations from the threat or use of force against the territorial integrity or political independence of any State.'

REVISION NOTE

The prohibition on the use of force is widely regarded to be a peremptory norm of modern international law. (See Chapter 2.)

What counts as a use of force?

Aggression

KEY DEFINITION: Aggression

Article 1: 'Aggression is the use of armed force by a state against the sovereignty, territorial integrity or political independence of another state, or in any manner inconsistent with the Charter of the United Nations . . .' Resolution on the Definition of Aggression, GA Resolution 29/3314 (1974).

Article 2 of the 1974 Resolution creates a presumption of aggression against the State proven to have been the first to use armed force.

Article 3, 1974 Resolution, identifies a range of acts of aggression, including:

- *Direct acts* – invasion, attack by armed forces and consequent military occupation; annexation by use of force, bombardment, blockade of ports.

- *Indirect acts* – sending of armed bands, groups, irregulars, mercenaries by one State to another which carry out acts of armed force of sufficient gravity.

EXAM TIP

According to the ICJ in the *Nicaragua Case* (1986), Article 3, 1974 Resolution reflects CIL. You should remind yourself of how CIL rules are formed. (See Chapter 2.)

Article 5, Rome Statute (1998), provides that the ICC has jurisdiction over crimes of aggression. However, such jurisdiction cannot be exercised until the Statute is amended to include a definition of the crime of aggression (the definition contained in the 1974 Resolution is widely regarded as unsuitable for the purpose of bringing prosecutions at the ICC). A definition was agreed and adopted by the parties to the ICC Statute at the Kampala Review Conference in 2010. However, the amendments to the Statute have yet to come into force.

📖 REVISION NOTE

A war of aggression is a crime against international peace, which gives rise to State responsibility (see Chapter 8). It is important to distinguish between State responsibility for a war of aggression and *individual* responsibility for war crimes or crimes against humanity which are liable to prosecution in the ICC.

Improper pressure and the use of force

Does economic or political pressure amount to a violation of Article 2(4) UN Charter?

In the *Nicaragua Case* (1986), the ICJ decided that economic sanctions directed at Nicaragua by the US did not amount to a breach of Article 2(4) UN Charter (see below).

While the use of improper pressure does not constitute a use of force in international law, if it induces a State to enter into a treaty it may be contrary to the UN Declaration on the Prohibition of Military, Political or Economic Coercion in the Conclusion of Treaties, adopted by the UN Conference on the Law of Treaties (1968–69). It arguably reflects CIL in this respect. Also see Article 52 VCLT (1969).

Threats

Is there a difference between a threat to use force and its actual use?

> The notions of 'threat' and 'use' of force . . . stand together in the sense that if the use of force in a given case is illegal . . . the threat to use such force will likewise be illegal. (*Legality of the Threat or Use of Nuclear Weapons Opinion* (1996) ICJ Rep 226, Para. 47)

 Make your answer stand out

International law may still be enforced by the traditional 'self-help' methods (an injured State enforces international law directly against a breaching State). Before the UN era, States were allowed to use force to enforce international law ('reprisals'). See the *Naulilaa Case (Portugal v Germany)* (1928) 2 RIAA 1011. However, the prohibition on the use of force means that reprisals are now unlawful. Does the prohibition on the use of force in modern international law undermine the concept of State sovereignty or the consent model of international law? You should consider the scope that still exists for non-coercive 'countermeasures' in international law.

> **!** **Don't be tempted to . . .**
>
> Don't be tempted to think that Article 2(4) prohibits the use of force in general. It is only concerned with the use of force in 'international relations'. It does not prohibit the use of force by States within their own territory. However, if a State uses force against its own people, other rights and obligations may be engaged. See the doctrine of humanitarian intervention, discussed below.

■ Exceptions to the prohibition on the use of force

Self-defence

KEY INSTRUMENT

Article 51, UN Charter

'Nothing in the present Charter shall impair the inherent right of individual or collective self-defence if an armed attack occurs against a Member of the United Nations . . .'

When does the right of self-defence arise?

KEY CASE

The Caroline Incident (1837) 29 BFSP 1137
Concerning: the right of self-defence in CIL

Facts

UK agents destroyed a US ship, *The Caroline*, which had been supplying rebels in Canada. The UK government claimed that it had acted in self-defence.

Legal principle

The US Secretary of State noted that the right of self-defence arises only in cases where there is 'a necessity of self-defence, instant, overwhelming, leaving no choice of means and no moment for deliberation [and involving] nothing unreasonable or excessive.'

✎ EXAM TIP

In the *Nicaragua Case* the ICJ confirmed that the reference to 'the inherent right of self-defence' contained in Article 51, UN Charter referred to the CIL right as developed by the *Caroline Incident*. This connection between CIL and treaty law in this regard shows how these sources work together to promote coherence and consistency in international law. (See Chapter 2.)

Make your answer stand out

The ICJ elaborated on concepts of necessity and proportionality in *Oil Platforms Case (Iran v USA)* (2003) ICJ Rep 161. It emphasised that the concept of necessity must be strictly construed and that it permits no scope for discretion. Moreover, it noted that the extent to which force is used in self-defence must be proportionate to the harm suffered (or to the risk of harm apparent in the circumstances).

What is an 'armed attack'?

KEY CASE

Nicaragua Case (Merits) (1986) ICJ Rep 14

Concerning: US support for paramilitary activities in Nicaragua
Legal issue: the meaning of an armed attack for the purpose of invoking a claim of self-defence

Facts

The US government provided logistical, supervisory and financial support to the Nicaraguan paramilitaries. The ICJ had to decide whether this conduct amounted to the use of force by the US. The US claimed that it was acting in collective self-defence.

Legal principle

The ICJ noted that self-defence can only be exercised in response to an armed attack. It recognised that an armed attack can be committed by regular armed forces or armed bands (but the latter must have achieved a threshold scale). However, it decided that an armed attack did not occur where logistical, supervisory and financial support was provided to armed forces.

□ REVISION NOTE

The *Caroline Incident* identified the CIL position concerning self-defence. The ICJ had to decide the *Nicaragua Case* by reference to CIL as it had no jurisdiction to apply the provisions of the UN Charter to resolve that dispute (see Chapter 9). It decided that the content of the relevant CIL rules and the UN Charter provisions concerning the prohibition on the use of force and self-defence were the same. (See Chapter 2.)

Make your answer stand out

What is the relationship between the 1974 GA Resolution and Article 2(4) UN Charter? Aggression is a narrower concept than the prohibition contained in Article 2(4). It is concerned with the use of armed force and it doesn't extend to threats to use force. Article 2(4) is more general in scope. It encompasses the provisions contained in the 1974 Resolution.

Duty to report acts undertaken in self-defence

KEY INSTRUMENT

Article 51, UN Charter

'Measures taken by Members . . . shall be immediately reported to the Security Council and shall not in any way affect the authority and responsibility of the Security Council under the present Charter . . .'

While Article 51 recognises the right of States to use force in self-defence it is important that the UNSC is immediately informed so that it can discharge its UN Charter responsibilities and maintain the integrity of the general prohibition on the use of force. This requirement underpins the view that the use of force can only be justified on an exceptional basis and that the ongoing use of force can only be lawful where it is sanctioned by the UNSC on behalf of the international community as a whole.

In the *Nicaragua Case* (1986), the ICJ observed that: 'the absence of a report may be one of the factors indicating whether the State in question was itself convinced that it was acting in self-defence' (Para. 200). However, it is important to note that this requirement relates to Article 51 and not the parallel CIL right.

Collective right of self-defence

The right of self-defence can be exercised either on an individual or a collective basis. For collective self-defence, there must be an expressed desire for assistance by the attacked State:

> there is no rule permitting the exercise of collective self-defence *in the absence of a request by the State which is a victim of the alleged attack*, this being additional to the requirement that the State in question should have declared itself to have been attacked. (*Nicaragua Case* (1986), Para. 199)

Collective self-defence arrangements have long been a feature of international relations. For example, see the NATO Treaty (1949). Article 5 provides that: 'The Parties agree that an armed attack against one or more of them in Europe or North America shall be considered an attack against them all . . .'

Anticipatory self-defence

Article 51 appears to limit the right of self-defence to situations where an armed attack has occurred. However, it has been claimed that States have a right to defend themselves before an armed attack occurs, if the threat is imminent. States cannot wait simply to be attacked especially by the kinds of weapon that are available today. This notion of anticipatory self-defence has been endorsed by the UN High Level Panel on Threats, Challenges and Change (2004).

 Don't be tempted to . . .

Don't confuse the concept of anticipatory self-defence with the idea of pre-emptive self-defence. The latter claims that a State has the right to attack before a hostile State develops the capacity to launch an attack at some point in the future. It was developed by the US government in its *National Security Strategy* (2002) 41 ILM 1478. This argument has not been supported by other States and thus it has no standing in international law.

Can the right of self-defence be used against non-State actors?

In the *Legal Consequences of the Construction of a Wall in the Occupied Palestinian Territory Opinion* (2004) ICJ Rep 136, Israel claimed that its actions were justified by Article 51 UN Charter (see Chapter 9). However, the ICJ decided that this provision: 'recognizes the existence of an inherent right of self-defence in the case of an armed attack by one State against another State' (Para. 139).

 Make your answer stand out

An 'armed attack' does not need to be committed by a State for the right of self-defence to be invoked. UNSC Res. 1368 (2001), which was passed in response to the 9/11 attacks on the US, recognised that the right of self-defence could be used to respond to terrorist attacks on a State. See Trapp (2007).

In the *Armed Activities Case (Congo v Uganda)* (2005) ICJ Rep 168, the ICJ recognised that there could be armed attacks by non-State actors in the absence of an effective governmental authority. However, where an act of aggression is committed by a non-State actor, an attack on a State pursuant to the right of self-defence can only be justified if that act of aggression is attributable to that State (see Chapter 8).

Actions expressly authorised by UNSC

Article 2(4) UN Charter prohibited the use of force, but does international law allow States to use force for good purposes?

UNSC is charged *inter alia* with the maintenance of international peace and security (Art. 24, UN Charter). It can enforce international legal rights and obligations by a variety of means (including through the use of force) if international peace and security is being threatened.

KEY INSTRUMENT

Chapter VII, UN Charter

Article 39: UNSC 'shall determine the existence of any threat to the peace, breach of the peace, or act of aggression and shall make recommendations or shall decide what measures shall be taken in accordance with Articles 41 and 42, to maintain or restore international peace and security.'

Article 42: UNSC 'may take such action by air, sea, or land forces as may be necessary to maintain or restore international peace and security. Such action may include demonstrations, blockade, and other operations by air, sea, or land forces of [UN] Members.'

KEY CASE

Invasion of Kuwait (1990)

Concerning: Iraq's unlawful invasion of Kuwait

Facts

Iraq invaded Kuwait in 1990. In response, UNSC adopted SC Resolution 660 (1990) which established that Iraq's actions constituted a breach of international peace and security.

Legal principle

In SC Resolution 662 (1990), UNSC decided that: '[The] annexation of Kuwait by Iraq under any form and whatever pretext has no legal validity, and is considered null and void.' Iraq's actions violated the prohibition on the use of force and the territorial integrity of an independent State contrary to Article 2(4) UN Charter and Principle 1 GA Res. 2625 (1970).

In SC Resolution 678 (1990), UNSC authorised the use of force against Iraq to compel the withdrawal of Iraq's forces and to restore regional peace and security. A coalition of 29 States began a military campaign, which quickly achieved these aims.

Figure 10.1
Operation of the right of self-defence

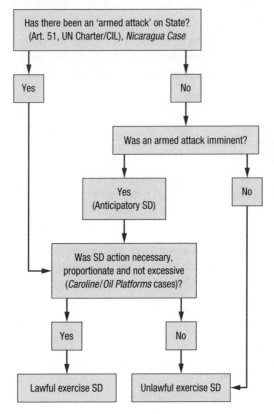

'Humanitarian' intervention/implied UNSC authorisation

Can States interfere in the domestic affairs of a sovereign State without the UNSC's express authorisation for good purposes (e.g. on humanitarian grounds)?

> **KEY INSTRUMENT**
>
> **Article 2(7), UN Charter**
>
> 'Nothing contained in the present Charter shall authorize the United Nations to intervene in matters which are essentially within the domestic jurisdiction of any State or shall require the Members to submit such matters to settlement under the present Charter . . .'

KEY CASE

NATO's intervention in Kosovo (1999)

Concerning: NATO's military intervention in Kosovo

Facts

The Federal Republic of Yugoslavia (FRY) used its armed forces to repress the ethnic Albanian inhabitants of Kosovo. In SC Resolution 1199 (1998), UNSC recognised that such actions threatened international peace and security. Although it demanded the immediate cessation of hostilities it did not authorise the use of force to achieve this purpose. In 1999, NATO mounted a bombing campaign which compelled the FRY's forces to withdraw from Kosovo.

Legal principle

It has been argued that NATO's actions were justified by the doctrine of humanitarian intervention, which holds that a targeted military intervention within a State is permissible to avert a humanitarian disaster that could not otherwise be avoided. However, some participating NATO member States preferred to justify its intervention by reference to implied authorisation from UNSC resolutions (see below).

Figure 10.2

Exceptions to prohibition on use of force

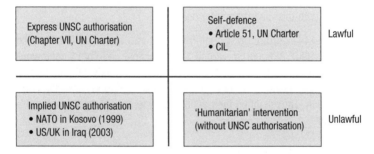

REVISION NOTE

It is important to remember the processes by which UNSC resolutions are made. In Kosovo, Russia (which was the FRY's closest ally) indicated that it would veto any proposal to adopt a resolution to authorise the use of force. It was Russia's threat to exercise its veto that led to NATO's decision to act without UNSC's authorisation. See Article 27, UN Charter.

If the UN Charter's provisions concerning collective security were rendered ineffective in Kosovo for political reasons what does this say about the effectiveness of international law in contested situations? It can be argued that NATO's intervention in Kosovo demonstrates that international law has a moral basis. However, it is difficult to reconcile this doctrine with the concept of State sovereignty and there is very little State practice in support of it (but see the coverage of the 'responsibility to protect' (below)).

✎ EXAM TIP

To what extent has UNSC Resolution 1973 (2011) which authorised NATO's limited intervention in Libya on humanitarian grounds strengthened the doctrine of humanitarian intervention? It would be a good idea to draw parallels between NATO's intervention in Kosovo and Libya.

KEY CASE

The US/UK invasion of Iraq (2003)

Concerning: the US/UK-led invasion of Iraq in 2003

Facts

Under SC Resolution 687 (1990), UNSC established a framework for the aftermath of the 1990 Gulf War. It dealt with (*inter alia*) the provisions for a ceasefire and it obligated Iraq to destroy its Weapons of Mass Destruction (WMDs) under UN supervision. Iraq failed to comply with this disarmament process.

In SC Resolution 1441 (2002), UNSC reaffirmed that Iraq was in material breach of SC Resolution 687 (1990). Although it warned that persistent non-compliance would have serious consequences, it gave Iraq a final opportunity to comply with its international legal obligations. Iraq failed to comply. In 2003, US and UK forces invaded Iraq without UNSC authorisation. They justified their actions by reference to Iraq's material breach of UNSC resolutions.

Legal principle

The UK claimed that, given the belief that Iraq possessed WMDs, by failing to disarm Iraq was in material breach of the ceasefire conditions contained in SC Resolution 687 (1990). Consequently, it argued that the authorisation contained in SC Resolution 678 (1990) was revived. However, UNSC remained seized of the situation at all material times and no resolution authorising the use of force was put forward. Moreover, the doctrine of implied authorisation has never been established in international law.

Make your answer stand out

Are there any parallels between the actions of NATO in Kosovo and those of the US/UK in Iraq in 2003? The US/UK claimed that their actions were partly in response to the Iraqi government's mistreatment of its own people. To what extent can humanitarian grounds be used to disguise other motives for intervention? Read Lowe (2003). You should reflect upon the dangers of the doctrine of humanitarian intervention for the concept of State sovereignty. A wide interpretation could render many States vulnerable to external intervention. Arguably, the existence of broad grounds for lawful intervention would cause a great deal of instability and undermine international order. But should international law seek to maintain an unjust peace? See Koskenniemi (2002).

Responsibility to protect (R2P)

The idea that States have a specific 'responsibility to protect' their nationals from a range of grave threats (including genocide, war crimes and crimes against humanity) was first advanced by the Canadian government in 2001. It supposes that if a State fails to discharge this responsibility then it is incumbent on the international community to discharge this obligation. R2P was subsequently endorsed by the UN General Assembly in its World Summit Outcome (GA Res. 60(1) (2005)). Further, R2P was developed by the UN Secretary-General in a 2009 Report.

📖 REVISION NOTE

R2P does not displace the current international legal regime concerning the grounds for military intervention, which depends on UNSC authorisation pursuant to Chapter VII, UN Charter. Does R2P amount to an international legal obligation or is it merely a political aspiration? See Zifcak (2010).

 Make your answer stand out

Arguably, the doctrines of humanitarian intervention and R2P have been compromised by the failure of the international community to intervene militarily in the ongoing Syrian civil war. How stable are such claimed international legal obligations if they depend on the political will of major States for their enforcement? (See Chapter 1 for more detail on this.)

■ Putting it all together

Answer guidelines

See the essay question at the start of the chapter.

Approaching the question

The question addresses the following areas:

- an overview of the history of the use of force in international law;
- prohibition on the use of force in modern international law;
- right of self-defence in international law;
- powers of the UNSC under Chapter VII, UN Charter;
- doctrine of humanitarian intervention.

Important points to include

- Briefly mention the role that the use of force/war played in international relations before the UN era and the justifications that exist for the prohibition on the use of force in modern international law.
- Outline the main elements of the prohibition on the use of force as identified in Article 2(4) UN Charter and the relevant sources of CIL (e.g. the 1974 General Assembly Resolution on Aggression).
- Focus on the exceptions to the prohibition on the use of force.
- Self-defence – you should discuss both the inherent right that has formed in CIL (e.g. *Caroline* and *Nicaragua*) and the treaty right contained in Article 51 UN Charter.
- Force used must be necessary and proportionate (*Caroline* and *Oil Platforms*).
- It should be in response to an armed attack (Art. 51) or an imminent armed attack.
- You should examine the collective dimension of the right (Art. 51, *Nicaragua*).
- Show that the right of self-defence exists within an institutional context (via the duty to report any act of self-defence to the UNSC immediately). It does not undermine the UNSC's mandate to maintain international peace and security. Consequently, you should emphasise the right's exceptional nature.
- Discuss the UNSC's powers under Chapter VII, UN Charter, and it would be useful to explore instances where the use of force has been authorised (e.g. Iraq 1990 and Libya 2011).

■ It is important to draw attention to the fact that the UNSC considers the use of force to be a measure of last resort and that it endeavours to resolve international disputes by peaceful means.

 Make your answer stand out

■ Discuss the extent to which the doctrine of humanitarian intervention is consistent with international law.

■ Explore the challenges for the doctrine presented by Article 2(4) and Article 2(7) UN Charter and the difficult cases that have emerged where the Security Council has not authorised the use of force under its Chapter VII powers. In this respect, you could compare and contrast the cases of Kosovo and Libya.

READ TO IMPRESS

Gray, C. (2003) 'The Use and Abuse of the International Court of Justice: Cases Concerning the Use of Force After Nicaragua', 14 *EJIL* 867.

Henderson, C. (2011) 'International Measure for the Protection of Civilians in Libya and Cote d'Ivoire', 60 *ICLQ* 767.

Koskenniemi, M. (2002) ' "The Lady Doth Protest Too Much": Kosovo, and the Turn to Ethics in International Law', 65 *MLR* 159.

Lowe, V. (2003) 'The Iraq Crisis: What Now?', 52 *ICLQ* 859.

Trapp, K. N. (2007) 'Back to Basics: Necessity, Proportionality, and the Right of Self-defence Against Non-State Actors', 57 *ICLQ* 141.

US National Security Strategy (2002) 41 *ILM* 1478.

Zifcak, S. (2010) 'The Responsibility to Protect', in M. Evans, *International Law*, 3rd edn. Oxford University Press.

www.pearsoned.co.uk/lawexpress

 Go online to access more revision support including quizzes to test your knowledge, sample questions with answer guidelines, podcasts you can download, and more!

And finally, before the exam . . .

The aim of this book is to help you to prepare for examinations in international law and much of the advice contained in it is specific to that subject. However, it is very important too that you remember a few *general* 'dos' and 'don'ts' which are sure to improve your performance in *any* exam.

Do remember to answer the set question (exams are not just a test of knowledge; you must *apply* the relevant law to the question). *Do* divide your time equally between the number of questions that you are supposed to answer (it is easier to get the first 50 per cent than the second!). *Do* use authority (primary and secondary sources) in support of your work. They will help to demonstrate your knowledge and understanding of the applicable law.

Don't get into the habit of citing authorities in brackets at the end of sentences (like a form of punctuation). Try to explain how a particular authority is relevant to your argument. *Don't* question-spot. Questions on your chosen topics may not come up (or they may not come up in the way that you had anticipated).

Test yourself

☐ Look at the **revision checklists** at the start of each chapter. Are you happy that you can now tick them all? If not, go back to the particular chapter and work through the material again. If you are still struggling, seek help from your tutor.

☐ Attempt the **sample questions** in each chapter and check your answers against the guidelines provided.

☐ Go online to **www.pearsoned.co.uk/lawexpress** for more hands-on revision help and try out these resources:

☐ Try the **test your knowledge** quizzes and see if you can score full marks for each chapter.

▶

☐ Attempt to answer the **sample questions** for each chapter within the time limit and check your answers against the guidelines provided.

☐ Listen to the **podcast** and then attempt the question it discusses.

☐ **'You be the marker'** and see if you can spot the strengths and weaknesses of the sample answers.

☐ Use the **flashcards** to test your recall of the legal principles of the key cases and statutes you've revised and the definitions of important terms.

☐ Keep up to date with **recent developments** in international law as this will enable you to demonstrate your understanding of international law by reference to topical examples, which may well earn you extra marks.

☐ Consider forming a **study group** with other students who are taking your international law module. Sometimes students can enhance their understanding of international law by discussing international legal issues with their peers.

☐ Don't forget to keep going back to the **primary and secondary sources** of international law (international instruments, cases and textbooks) to check your understanding of key legal issues as this will reinforce and consolidate your learning.

■ Linking it all up

You should develop your understanding of how the sources of international law (CIL and treaty law) work together to create or change international law. Consequently, you need to appreciate how these sources relate to one another. Revise Chapters 2 and 3.

Questions about the source of a particular rule of international law and the ways in which CIL rules and treaty rules work in a specific area are popular (e.g. see consideration of the international law concerning the use of force in the *Nicaragua Case* (1986)). These are the building blocks of international law and so it is important that you acquire a good understanding of them. See Chapters 2 and 10.

If a State has breached international law then the question of whether it bears international responsibility for its acts/omissions will invariably arise. You should always be prepared to consider whether a particular act or omission would give rise to State responsibility. The topic of State responsibility is covered in Chapter 8.

The topics of State jurisdiction and State immunity are closely interrelated. Both topics are essential to an international legal system that is premised on the concept of sovereignty – the exercise of jurisdiction is a manifestation of a State's sovereign authority while a State's right to immunity from an exercise of jurisdiction by another State is also central to the notion of sovereignty. See Chapter 6.

Check where there are overlaps between subject areas. (You may want to review the 'Revision note' boxes throughout this book.) Make a careful note of these as knowing how one topic may lead into another can increase your marks significantly. Here are some examples:

✔ The international law regulating continental shelf claims demonstrates how treaty law and CIL work together to develop international law. See the *North Sea Continental Shelf Cases* (1969). Read Chapters 2 and 3.

✔ A State that commits a material breach of a binding treaty will invariably bear international responsibility for that breach of international law. See the *Rainbow Warrior Case* (1987). Read Chapters 3 and 8.

✔ A State that exercises its jurisdiction over a serving Head of State or Foreign Minister of another State would prompt a claim of State immunity and it would give rise to a claim of State responsibility as well. See the *Pinochet Case* (2000) and the *Arrest Warrant Case* (2002). Read Chapters 6 and 8.

▮ Knowing your cases

Make sure you know how to use relevant examples of international law in your answers. Use the table below to focus your revision of the key example in each topic. To review the details of these examples, refer back to the particular chapter.

Key examples	How to use	Related topics
Chapter 1 – Nature of international law		
Lotus Case (1927)	To show that international law is grounded in State consent	State jurisdiction
Chapter 2 – Sources of international law		
North Sea Continental Shelf Cases (1969)	To show how CIL is formed	Law of treaties; customary international law
Anglo-Norwegian Fisheries Case (1951)	To show the operation of the persistent objector rule in relation to the formation of CIL rules	The consent model of international law

▶

Key examples	How to use	Related topics
Nicaragua Case (Merits) (1986)	To show the relationship between CIL and treaties in the context of the use of force and the right of self-defence	State responsibility; use of force; self-defence

Chapter 3 – Treaties

Key examples	How to use	Related topics
Maritime Delimitation & Territorial Questions Case (Jurisdiction) (1994)	To show what counts as a treaty for the purposes of international law	The nature and extent of ICJ jurisdiction
Anglo-French Continental Shelf Case (1977)	To show the effect of valid treaty reservations on international legal rights and obligations	
Territorial Dispute (Libya/Chad) (1994)	To show how treaties are interpreted	Acquisition of ICJ jurisdiction; jurisdictional clauses; territorial disputes
Namibia Opinion (1971)	To show how treaty interpretation can be influenced by subsequent developments in international law To show the legal consequences of a material breach of a treaty	Self-determination; ICJ Advisory Opinions
Cameroon v *Nigeria Case* (2002)	To illustrate the relative grounds for invalidating a treaty	The relationship between international law and national law
Gabcikovo-Nagymaros Case (1997)	To show the legal consequences of a material breach of a treaty To illustrate the grounds for terminating a treaty (the grounds of supervening impossibility and fundamental change of circumstances)	State responsibility

Key examples	How to use	Related topics
	To show the relationship between treaty breaches and State responsibility (via the defence of necessity)	
Fisheries Jurisdiction Case (1973)	To illustrate the grounds for terminating a treaty (fundamental change of circumstances)	State responsibility
Rainbow Warrior Case (1987)	To show the relationship between treaty breaches and State responsibility (via the defence of *force majeure*)	State responsibility
Chapter 4 – International legal personality		
Austro-German Customs Union Case (1931)	To show the interpretation of 'independence' as a criterion of statehood with regard to an established State	Self-determination
The Aaland Islands Case (1920)	To show the interpretation of 'independence' as a criterion of statehood with regard to a new State	Self-determination
Congo's Independence (1960)	To show how the exercise of the right to self-determination in situations of decolonisation can lead to the relaxation of test for statehood	Self-determination
Manchukuo (1931–3)	To show the operation of the doctrine of non-recognition of States	Self-determination
Southern Rhodesia (1965)	To show the operation of the doctrine of non-recognition of States	Self-determination
Bosnia-Herzegovina (1991–1995)	To show how the international community can support a claim to statehood by according recognition despite the claimant entity's inability to satisfy the Montevideo criteria	Self-determination
Kosovo's Declaration of Independence (2008)	To show how the international community can support a claim to statehood by according recognition despite the claimant entity's inability to satisfy the Montevideo criteria	Self-determination

▶

Key examples	How to use	Related topics
EC Guidelines on the Recognition of New States in Eastern Europe and USSR (1991)	To show the requirements for recognising new States as a matter of international law	Self-determination
Reparations Advisory Opinion (1949)	To show how an IGO can acquire international legal personality	Judicial dispute resolution
Chapter 5 – International law and national law		
R v *Keyn* (1876–7)	To show the relationship between CIL and UK law in the context of jurisdiction	State jurisdiction
Mortensen v *Peters* (1906)	To show the relationship between CIL and UK law in the context of jurisdiction	State jurisdiction
Trendtex Trading v *Central Bank of Nigeria* (1977)	To show the relationship between CIL and UK law in respect of claims of State immunity in civil matters	State immunity
R v *Margaret Jones and Others* (2007)	To show whether CIL can be used as a defence to criminal charges under UK law	State jurisdiction
The Parlement Belge (1879–80)	To show that a treaty must be transformed into national law by statute if it is to be considered justiciable in the UK courts	State immunity
Maclaine Watson v *DTI* (1990)	To examine whether the UK could be liable for the debts of an IGO created by a treaty as a matter of UK law	International legal personality
R v *Secretary of State Home Department, ex parte Brind* (1991)	To consider whether an untransformed treaty could be justiciable in the UK courts	State jurisdiction
Alabama Arbitration (1872)	To show that State responsibility can arise where national law is inconsistent with a State's international legal obligations	State responsibility; judicial dispute resolution

Key examples	How to use	Related topics
Cameroon v *Nigeria* (2002)	To show that a State cannot invoke the provisions of its national law to avoid international legal obligations	Grounds for invalidating a treaty
Chapter 6 – Jurisdiction and immunity		
Lotus Case (1927)	To show the nature and extent of prescriptive and enforcement jurisdiction	The consent model of international law
Al-Skeini v *UK* (2011)	To demonstrate the operation of the principle of extraterritorial jurisdiction	The law of treaties
Lockerbie Prosecutions (2001)	To demonstrate the exercise of the objective territorial principle of jurisdiction	Judicial dispute resolution
A-G of Israel v *Eichmann* (1961)	To show the operation of the universal and protective principles of jurisdiction	
Arrest Warrant Case (2002)	To show the limits of universal jurisdiction and the operation of the doctrine of State immunity	State responsibility
DPP v *Joyce* (1946)	To show the operation of the protective principle of jurisdiction	
Cutting's Case (1886)	To show the limits of a claim of jurisdiction under the passive personality principle of jurisdiction	
US v *Yunis (No. 2)* (1991)	To show that a claim of jurisdiction under the passive personality principle can be legitimate in exceptional circumstances	
R v *Bow Street Magistrates, ex parte Pinochet (No. 3)* (2000)	To show the operation of the nature and extent of the doctrine of State immunity in criminal proceedings	Relationship between international law and national law
The Parlement Belge (1879–80)	To illustrate the nature and extent of claims of immunity from State jurisdiction in civil matters	The doctrine of transformation

▶

Key examples	How to use	Related topics
Germany v *Italy (Jurisdictional Immunities of States)* (2012)	To show the extent to which States enjoy immunity from the civil jurisdiction of the national courts of other States	State responsibility
Trendtex Trading v *Central Bank of Nigeria* (1977)	To illustrate the limits of claims of immunity from State jurisdiction regarding civil matters	The doctrine of incorporation
US Diplomatic and Consular Staff in Tehran (1980)	To show the nature and extent of diplomatic immunity in international law	State responsibility
Julian Assange Case (2012)	To explore the limits of diplomatic immunity and asylum	The relationship between international law and national law

Chapter 7 – Territory and self-determination

Island of Palmas Case (1928)	To show how title to territory can be acquired in international law (especially via occupation and prescription)	The concepts of sovereignty and jurisdiction
	To show the relative nature of the exercise of sovereign authority over territory	
Eastern Greenland Case (1933)	To show the acquisition of title to territory in international law (especially via occupation and prescription)	Judicial dispute resolution
Clipperton Island Arbitration (1932)	To show the sovereign acts required to support a claim of territorial acquisition in respect of uninhabited territory	
Frontier Dispute (1986)	To show the nature of the principle of *uti possidetis*	
	To show that the *uti possidetis* principle is not restricted to instances of decolonisation	Relationship between the principles of *uti possidetis*, self-determination and statehood

Key examples	How to use	Related topics
Wall Opinion (2004)	To illustrate the nature and extent of the right to self-determination in international law	Judicial dispute resolution; State responsibility
Re Secession of Quebec (1998)	To illustrate the nature of the right to self-determination	The sources of international law
Palestine's Claim to Statehood (2012)	To explore the creation and recognition of States in international law	International legal personality
Dissolution of Yugoslavia (1990–91)	To explore the relationship between self-determination, recognition and statehood in situations of State dissolution	Recognition of new States
	To illustrate the relationship between the principles of self-determination and *uti possidetis* in international law	

Chapter 8 – State responsibility and diplomatic protection

Key examples	How to use	Related topics
Corfu Channel Case (1949)	To show that a State can be internationally responsible for its failure to prevent a breach of international law	Judicial dispute resolution
Caire Claim (1929)	To show how States can be responsible for the *ultra vires* acts of their officials	
Nicaragua Case (Merits) (1986)	To explore whether States can be responsible for the actions of paramilitary groups	Creation of CIL; use of force; self-defence
Rainbow Warrior Case (1987)	To show the relationship between treaty breaches and State responsibility (via the defence of *force majeure*)	Treaty termination
Gabcikovo-Nagymaros Case (1997)	To show the relationship between treaty breaches and State responsibility (via the defence of necessity)	Treaty termination
Nottebohm Case (1955)	To show the circumstances in which a State can exercise diplomatic protection on behalf of one of its nationals	State jurisdiction

▶

Key examples	How to use	Related topics
Barcelona Traction Case (1970)	To show the limits to the exercise of the right of diplomatic protection	*Jus cogens* and obligations *erga omnes*
Mavrommatis Palestine Concession Case (1924)	To show the nature of the right of diplomatic protection	State jurisdiction
BP v *Libya Arbitration* (1974)	To illustrate the international legal requirements concerning the treatment of aliens (expropriation of property)	
Aminoil v *Kuwait* (1982)	To illustrate the international legal requirements concerning the treatment of aliens (expropriation of property)	
Diallo Case (2010)	To illustrate the international legal requirements concerning the treatment of aliens (human rights)	Development of human rights in modern international law
Chorzow Factory Case (1928)	To show the nature and purpose of reparations when State responsibility is established	
'I'm Alone' Case (1933–35)	To show the forms and extent of reparations in the event of a finding of State responsibility	
Robert E Brown Case (1923)	To examine whether local remedies need to be exhausted for a valid claim of State responsibility to arise	
ELSI Case (1989)	To consider the scope of the local remedies doctrine in relation to State responsibility	

Chapter 9 – Judicial dispute resolution

Nicaragua Case (Jurisdiction) (1984)	To illustrate the operation of the optional clause under Article 36(2) ICJ Statute	Creation of CIL; use of force; self-defence; State responsibility

Key examples	How to use	Related topics
	To show the way in which a reservation can restrict the ICJ's jurisdiction to determine an international legal dispute	
La Grand (Provisional Measures) (1999)	To show the binding nature of provisional measures as a matter of international law	International legal personality
Maritime Delimitation & Territorial Questions (Jurisdiction) Case (1994)	To show the basis for ICJ jurisdiction via special agreements	The nature of a treaty
Territorial Dispute (Libya v *Chad)* (1994)	To show the basis for ICJ jurisdiction via a jurisdictional clause in a treaty	Treaty interpretation; title to territory
Certain Questions of Mutual Assistance (Djibouti v *France)* (2008)	To show the basis for ICJ jurisdiction via the principle of *forum prorogatum*	
Rights of Passage Case (Preliminary Objections) (1957)	To establish when ICJ jurisdiction can arise under the optional clause (Art. 36(2) ICJ Statute)	Nature of CIL
Norwegian Loans Case (1957)	To show how reservations have a reciprocal effect for the purpose of international litigation	State responsibility and diplomatic protection
Lockerbie Case (Libya v *US/UK) (Provisional Measures)* (1992)	The relationship between the ICJ and UNSC. To consider whether the ICJ has the power to review UNSC decisions	
Nuclear Weapons Opinion (1996)	To examine the relationship between international human rights law and international humanitarian law in the context of the use of nuclear weapons	Sources of international law

▶

Key examples	How to use	Related topics
	To demonstrate the nature and significance of the ICJ's Advisory Jurisdiction	
Wall Opinion (2004)	To show the circumstances in which UNGA can request an Advisory Opinion	Self-determination; State responsibility
	To demonstrate the nature and significance of Advisory Opinions	
Kosovo Opinion (2010)	To demonstrate the nature and effect of ICJ Advisory Opinions	Recognition of new States
	To consider the validity of a unilateral declaration of independence as a matter of international law	

Chapter 10 – Use of force

Caroline Incident (1837)	To show the requirements of a lawful act of self-defence in CIL	Formation of CIL
Nicaragua Case (Merits) (1986)	To establish the meaning of an armed attack for the purpose of invoking a claim of self-defence	Creation of CIL; State responsibility; ICJ jurisdiction
	To explore the prohibition on the use of force in international law, the right of self-defence and the relationship between the provisions of the UN Charter and CIL	
Invasion of Kuwait (1990)	To show how the UNSC authorises the use of force pursuant to its Chapter VII powers	Nature of international law
NATO's intervention in Kosovo (1999)	To consider whether the use of force can be lawful in the absence of express UNSC authorisation	Nature of international law
	To examine the doctrine of humanitarian intervention	
	To illustrate the limits of the notion of collective defence	

Key examples	How to use	Related topics
Invasion of Iraq (2003)	To consider whether the use of force can be lawful in the absence of express UNSC authorisation	Nature of international law
	To examine the doctrine of humanitarian intervention	

■ Sample question

Below is an essay question that incorporates overlapping areas of the law. See if you can answer this question drawing upon your knowledge of the whole subject area. Guidelines on answering this question are included at the end of this section.

ESSAY QUESTION

Analyse the contribution that the ICJ's judgment in the *Arrest Warrant Case (Democratic Republic of the Congo* v *Belgium)* (2002) has made to the following areas of international law:

(a) the notion of 'universal jurisdiction'; and

(b) the international law concerning State immunity.

Both parts carry equal marks.

Answer guidelines

Approaching the question

This question requires you to analyse two significant and overlapping issues that confronted the ICJ in the *Arrest Warrant Case* (2002).

To answer it you will need to acquire a comprehensive understanding of the universal principle of State jurisdiction and the nature and extent to which a State can claim immunity from a claim of jurisdiction by another State. ▶

Important points to include

Part (a) invites you to reflect upon the extent to which the notion of universal jurisdiction is entrenched in the ICJ's jurisprudence.

- You should briefly discuss the bases of jurisdiction and the justification for universal jurisdiction given the absence of a World Court endowed with compulsory jurisdiction (e.g. *Eichmann*).

- You could also discuss the quasi-universal approach adopted in certain multilateral treaties (e.g. *Pinochet Case*).

- You should examine the Joint Separate Opinion of Judges Koojimans, Higgins and Buergenthal in the *Arrest Warrant Case*.

Part (b) focuses on the State immunity aspects of the *Arrest Warrant Case*.

- You should pay particular attention to the distinction between personal and functional immunity.

- The case drew upon the immunity recognised in respect of Heads of State (see *Pinochet*) which arose from an analogy itself with the position international law has adopted in relation to serving diplomats and it extended that protection to serving Foreign Ministers.

You should link the topics of State jurisdiction and State immunity together by exploring the way in which they demonstrate the operation of the concept of State sovereignty.

 Make your answer stand out

In relation to part (a), you should explore the dangers of the exercise of universal jurisdiction by States, as identified in the Separate Opinion of the ICJ President in the *Arrest Warrant Case*.

In contrast, you could consider the extent to which international tribunals can exercise universal jurisdiction on behalf of the international community (e.g. the ICC's jurisdiction).

Regarding part (b), you should reflect on how far immunity should extend and you might also consider the ethical and practical considerations involved in claims of State immunity.

You should also consider the circumstances in which a claim of jurisdiction could give rise to State responsibility (Belgium was held to be responsible for its actions in the *Arrest Warrant Case*).

Glossary of terms

The glossary is divided into two parts: key definitions and other useful terms. The key definitions can be found within the chapter in which they occur as well as in the glossary below. These definitions are the essential terms that you must know and understand in order to prepare for an exam. The additional list of terms provides further definitions of useful terms and phrases which will also help you answer examination and coursework questions effectively. These terms are highlighted in the text as they occur but the definitions can only be found here.

■ Key definitions

Aggression	Article 1: 'Aggression is the use of armed force by a state against the sovereignty, territorial integrity or political independence of another state, or in any manner inconsistent with the Charter of the United Nations . . .' Resolution on the Definition of Aggression, GA Resolution 29/3314 (1974).
Annexation	Annexation occurs where one State uses force to acquire territory belonging to another State.
Arbitration	'a procedure for the settlement of disputes between states by a binding award on the basis of law and as a result of an undertaking voluntarily accepted.' ILC Report (1953).
Cession	Cession occurs where territory is transferred from one State to another State by treaty.
Constitutive theory of recognition	It is the act of recognition by other States that creates the new State by endowing it with legal existence. A new State is created by the will of existing States.
Custom	'Custom is . . . established by virtue of a pattern of claim, absence of protest by states particularly interested in the matter at hand and acquiescence by other states.' Shaw (2008), 89.

Customary international law (CIL)

CIL has been defined as 'a constant and uniform usage, accepted as law'. (*Asylum Case* (1950) ICJ Rep 266, 277).

Declaratory theory of recognition

'the existence or disappearance of the State is a question of fact . . . the effects of recognition are purely declaratory' – Opinion No. 1, EC Arbitration Commission on Yugoslavia (1991) 31 ILM 1494.

Diplomatic protection

A State has the right to invoke: 'through diplomatic action or other means of peaceful settlement, of the responsibility of another State for an injury caused by an internationally wrongful act of that State to a natural or legal person that is a national of the former State with a view to the implementation of such responsibility.' Article 1 ILC Draft Articles on Diplomatic Protection 2006 (DADP).

Dualism

International law and national law constitute entirely separate legal systems.

Enforcement jurisdiction

Enforcement jurisdiction concerns a State's capacity to enforce its national laws in its own territory.

General principles of law

Article 38(1)(c) ICJ Statute: 'the general principles of law recognised by civilised nations'.

Immunity *ratione materiae*

Former Heads of State are entitled to functional immunity from the exercise of criminal jurisdiction by the courts of another State in certain situations.

Immunity *ratione personae*

Serving Heads of State enjoy absolute immunity from the exercise of criminal jurisdiction by the courts of another State.

Incorporation

International law is *automatically* part of national law. In principle, a national court is bound to apply international legal rules where they are relevant to a case before it.

International law

' . . . a body of rules and principles that determine the rights and duties of states primarily in respect of their dealing with other states and the citizens of other states.' Lowe (2007), 5.

International legal personality

'A subject of the law is an entity capable of possessing international rights and duties and having the capacity to maintain its rights by bringing international claims.' *Reparations Case* (1949) ICJ Rep 174.

'Material breach'

Article 60(3) VCLT, a material breach as one that is:

(a) a repudiation of the treaty not sanctioned by the VCLT; or

(b) the violation of a provision essential to the accomplishment of the object or purpose of the treaty.

Monism	International law and national law are components of a single legal system.
Occupation	Occupation arises where a piece of territory is settled and claimed on behalf of a State.
Objective territorial principle	The objective territorial principle holds that a State has jurisdiction over a criminal offence that has been completed within its territory.
Opinio juris	It is necessary that States believe that they are under a legal obligation to follow a particular practice.
Prescription	Prescription occurs where a State acquires title to territory by successfully displacing the sovereign authority of a State that has previously claimed sovereignty over that territory.
Prescriptive jurisdiction	Prescriptive jurisdiction is concerned with a State's capacity to legislate for certain persons and in certain situations.
Purpose of recognition	'The purpose of recognition is to endow the new entity with capacity vis-à-vis the recognising State, to be a bearer of rights and duties under international law and participate in international relations on the footing of international law.' Schwarzenberger (1976).
Reparations	'Responsibility is the necessary corollary of a right. All rights of an international character involve international responsibility. If the obligation in question is not met, responsibility entails the duty to make reparation.' Huber J in *Spanish Zones of Morocco Claims* (1925) 2 RIAA 615, 641.
Self-determination	The principle that all peoples have the right to freely determine their political status and to pursue economic, social and cultural development.
Subjects of international law	'The subjects of law in any legal system are not necessarily identical in their nature or in the extent of their rights, and their nature depends upon the needs of the community . . .' *Reparations Case* (1949) ICJ Rep 174.
Subjective territorial principle	The subjective territorial principle holds that a State has criminal jurisdiction in relation to an offence that was commenced in its territory but completed in the territory of another State.
Territorial sovereignty	'Sovereignty in the relations between States signifies independence. Independence in regard to a portion of the globe is the right to exercise therein, to the exclusion of any other State, the functions of the State.' Huber J in the *Island of Palmas Case* (1928) 22 AJIL 867, 838.

Transformation	International law only becomes part of national law if something is done to transform it into national law (either by enacting national legislation which gives effect to an international legal rule in national law or the decision of the national courts).
Treaties	Treaties are legally binding agreements that commit the parties to follow a particular course of conduct by reference to rights and/or obligations. Article 2(2) Vienna Convention on the Law of Treaties (VCLT) (1969) defines a treaty as an: 'international agreement concluded between States in written form and governed by international law'.
Ubi societas, ubi jus	'Law can only exist in a society, and there can be no society without a system of law to regulate the relations of its members with one another.' Brierly (1963), 41.
Uti possidetis juris	'New States will come to independence with the same boundaries they had when they were administrative units within the territory or territories of a colonial power.' Shaw (1996) 97.

■ Other useful terms

AJIL	American Journal of International Law.
BYIL	British Yearbook of International Law.
ECHR	European Convention on Human Rights.
EJIL	European Journal of International Law.
ICC	International Criminal Court.
ICJ	International Court of Justice.
ICLQ	International and Comparative Law Quarterly.
IGOs	International governmental organisations.
ILC	International Law Commission.
ILM	International Legal Materials.
MLR	Modern Law Review.
Jus cogens	Norms that have acquired a higher status in international law because they are widely seen as being of fundamental importance to the international legal system.
***Lotus* principle**	The actions of States are presumed to be lawful unless they have been specifically prohibited by international law.

Non-liquet	The absence of a legal rule to resolve a particular legal dispute, which would lead an international court to decline jurisdiction to determine the case.
Obligations *erga omnes*	Obligations owed to all States in international law.
Persistent objector rule	If a State objects to a new CIL rule from the moment it is established and it maintains its objection then the State will not be bound by that rule.
Ratification	A signal that a State is willing to be bound by a treaty.
Treaty reservation	Where a State makes a declaration that purports to modify its obligations as a party to that treaty.

Index